Pro Bono?

Pro Bono?

Mikkel Thorup

Winchester, UK
Washington, USA

First published by Zero Books, 2015
Zero Books is an imprint of John Hunt Publishing Ltd., Laurel House, Station Approach,
Alresford, Hants, SO24 9JH, UK
office1@jhpbooks.net
www.johnhuntpublishing.com
www.zero-books.net

For distributor details and how to order please visit the 'Ordering' section on our website.

Text copyright: Mikkel Thorup 2014

ISBN: 978 1 78279 867 5
Library of Congress Control Number: 2015933780

A CIP catalogue record for this book is available from the British Library.

Design: Lee Nash

Printed and bound by CPI Group (UK) Ltd, Croydon, CR0 4YY, UK

We operate a distinctive and ethical publishing philosophy in all
areas of our business, from our global network of authors to
production and worldwide distribution.

CONTENTS

1

The Soul of Humankind under Philanthropic Capitalism

Just a few years apart but on each side of the Atlantic, two essays on inequality and philanthropy were published. The first, published in 1889 by the enormously rich American businessman Andrew Carnegie, was entitled "Gospel of Wealth" and was addressed to the rich and mighty. The second was by the Irish poet and writer Oscar Wilde, who in 1891 published "The Soul of Man under Socialism" as an indictment of private property. The first essay is constantly and positively mentioned and cited in today's talk of a philanthropic capitalism. The second one is hardly ever noticed, but that is the one of the two that speaks the truth.

Carnegie's "Gospel of Wealth" is basically a reflection on how to sustain inequality in a time of socialist and anarchist threat to private property. It is an instalment of feudal-like social relations in an age of individualism. "The problem of our age", he starts the essay, "is the proper administration of wealth, so that the ties of brotherhood may still bind together the rich and poor in harmonious relationship." (Carnegie 2006, 1) The condition of inequality is taken for granted, it is even taken as a measure of civilization, and the question is therefore, how the rich are to relate to and paternalistically help the poor. Capitalist competition that condemns the many to a precarious existence and rewards the few "is best for the race, because it ensures the survival of the fittest in every department." (Ibid., 3) He then enlists all his readers – or just the very rich? – by saying: "We accept and welcome therefore, as conditions to which we must accommodate ourselves, great inequality of environment, the concentration of business, industrial and commercial, in the hands of a few, and the law of competition between these, as being not only beneficial, but essential for the future progress of the race." (Ibid.) One gets the feeling that these are sentiments of inequality's virtues rather than the philanthropic thoughts that are the real appeal to present-day philanthropists.

The immediate reason for the essay is not really the plight of the poor but the threat from "the Socialist and Anarchist who seeks to overturn present conditions", threats which attack "the sacredness of property [on which] civilization itself depends – the right of the laborer to his hundred dollars in the savings-bank, and equally the legal right of the millionaire to his millions." (Ibid., 4) Therefore, inequality is not bad in itself. It is a sign of progress and civilization as well as the reward to "those who have the ability and energy" to accumulate riches (Ibid.). The deservedly rich have a number of ways of administering their wealth and Carnegie heaps scorn on giving it away after one's death either to relatives or to public purposes:

> There remains, then, only one mode of using great fortunes; but in this we have the true antidote for the temporary unequal distribution of wealth, the reconciliation of the rich and the poor – a reign of harmony – another ideal, differing, indeed, from that of the Communist in requiring only the further evolution of existing conditions, not the total overthrow of our civilization. (Ibid., 8)

Carnegie's idea is basically a re-feudalization, a social hierarchy that he earlier in the essay had lamented is no longer possible to exercise in the great industrial plants. Now, it re-emerges as 'help to the poor'. The dichotomization of the social is taken as a given, no value is bestowed on redistribution, and the wealthy giver is cast as the only one able to properly understand and administer the common good:

> Under its sway, we shall have an ideal state, in which the surplus wealth of the few will become, in the best sense, the property of the

many, because administered for the common good, and this wealth, passing through the hands of the few, can be a much more potent force for the elevation of our race than if it had been distributed in small sums to the people themselves. (Ibid.)

Redistribution would just mean a squandering of money, spent on the usual indulgencies and excesses of the poor. No, better to spend the money on museums, parks, libraries and the like (still a dominant way of 'charity' but one looked uneasily upon by the philanthropic capitalists who we are to describe below). This kind of philanthropic activity locks in economic and social inequality. The millionaire has "superior wisdom, experience, and ability to administer, doing for [the poor] better than they would or could do for themselves." (Ibid. 10) He is installed, like the feudal lord, as a "trustee for the poor." (Ibid., 12) Today, one cannot speak this neo-feudal language explicitly, but I will argue hereunder that the same juggling between economic and social inequality is what is at stake in philanthropic capitalism.

Perhaps Oscar Wilde had read Carnegie's essay. It appeared in the English *Pall Mall Gazette* shortly after its American printing, and Wilde's piece is a perfect antidote to the benign paternalism of Carnegie, inspired as it is by the very same political ideas that Carnegie defined his position against. Wilde acknowledges how people "with admirable though misdirected intentions [...] very seriously and very sentimentally set themselves the task of remedying the evils that they see. But their remedies do not cure the disease: they merely prolong it. Indeed, their remedies are part of the disease." (Wilde 1904, 4-5) The latter comment will be part of the argument throughout this book. Rather than alleviate – or entertain, as in the case of Carnegie – the poor, the *"proper aim is to try and reconstruct society on such a basis that poverty will be impossible.* And the altruistic virtues have really prevented the carrying out of this aim." (Ibid., 5) Their altruistic activities and understanding serve as a way to blind themselves as to the

3

causes of poverty as well as to blind and pacify those reserving the help:

> *Just as the worst slave-owners were those who were kind to their slaves, and so prevented the horror of the system being realized by those who suffered from it, and understood by those who contemplated it, so, in the present state of things in England, the people who do most harm are the people who try to do most good.* (Ibid)

The poor, Wilde says, take charity "to be a ridiculously inadequate mode of partial restitution, or a sentimental dole, usually accompanied by some impertinent attempt on the part of the sentimentalist to tyrannize over their private lives" (Ibid., 10-11); something easily recognizable today in both charity and welfare systems. It is "both immoral and unfair" (Ibid., 6) to help the poor with wealth gained from a system dependent upon the unequal position of people, but it is even worse to expect gratitude from people 'helped'. "We are often told", he says, "that the poor are grateful for charity. Some of them are no doubt, *but the best amongst the poor are never grateful*. They are ungrateful, discontented, disobedient, and rebellious." (Ibid., 10) It is that attitude to philanthropic capitalism that we will try to use and cultivate in the chapters to follow; a shedding of, not exactly gratitude, but praise of the philanthropists; a disobedience to the celebration of the rich helping the poor; and with that a realignment of the battle lines between the rich and the rest, and between the present system and the solution.

What to make, for instance, of Jeffrey Sachs speaking out in favor of the bottom one billion of the population forgotten by the constant top-X lists of the world's richest/most influential … (Sachs 2007; on Sachs see Klein 2007; Munk 2013; Wilson 2014a) Seemingly welcome attention. Making the case for a "Forbes One Billion" of the poor, we get a glimpse into the skewed attention of philanthropic capitalists. Sachs rightly says that if "journalists spent as much time studying the lives of the poor as they do gazing at the rich, it would help us all keep our heads on straight. We would marvel at a world economy strange enough to sustain such gaps" between rich and poor. All good and true, but then he continues: "We'd learn not to blame the rich for the poverty of the poor, but we'd also learn not to blame the poor themselves. Blame is a primitive response." Is it really? In a world of such glaring inequalities and injustices, is blame really inappropriate? Leaving aside the thorny question of not blaming the poor – thereby taking away all their agency and responsibility – and just concentrating on the rich, why shouldn't we all blame them for not only profiting from but actively helping to sustain the world such as it is? Ok then, if blame, meaning responsibility, is not the way forward, then what is: "Entrepreneurship is a much better one. The Forbes 400 could do an amazing job to help The Forbes One Billion into the world economy." There it is; the identified and named 400 to help the unidentified anonymous mass of poor people. Inequality doubled. Not only do the 400 own more than the one billion, now they must also suffer the indignity of having Sachs proclaiming the few the saviors of the many.

The 'no blame' game continues: "Americans learn from The Forbes 400 that the rich by and large didn't make it by monopolies, inheritance or government largesse. They were often very creative, very hardworking and extremely lucky in riding the crest of globalization, finance and information technologies." So, no questioning the system or its profiteers. Lucrative tax breaks, odious speculation, questionable business methods, crime and corruption apparently had nothing to do with today's super-rich. We should also, Sachs says, learn from the Forbes One Billion that the poor and the African governments are not to blame. Rather, the blame is on "soils depleted of nutrients, lack of infrastructure, malaria and drought. The Forbes One Billion will help us to see extreme poverty as a global anomaly often resulting from extremes of geography as well as extremes of historical bad luck." The impersonal forces of geography and bad luck rather than trade agreements, predatory lending, structural adjustment programs, corruption, neoliberalism etc. are why some people are poor, while individual entrepreneurship and creativity is the reason why very few people are extremely rich.

"Now, what if Forbes can also arrange for the Forbes billionaires to meet the Forbes One Billion?" The super-rich are the solution, not the problem obviously. The way Sachs describes the billionaire philanthropists, one should think that no one else has ever taken up the plight of the poor, least of all the poor themselves. "Bill Gates is today's Rockefeller, taking on AIDS, tuberculosis and malaria in hand-to-hand combat with new drugs, new vaccines, new diagnostics, new delivery system." Gates is out there alone in hand-to-hand combat with the symptoms of poverty. No one else apparently, no governments, NGOs, church groups, activists, community organizations or suchlike, prompting Sachs to ask: "Who else will take up the antipoverty challenge? There are life-and-death problems to occupy the best of the world's creative minds."

To think that the world's creative minds are exclusively or even predominantly to be found in private business or among the super-rich is incredible. To expect change that will transform the condition of inequality of today's capitalist system coming from the ones gaining most from that system is even harder to fathom. To think that is to be the contemporary equivalent of the apologist for slavery who references the good-hearted slave owner and who implores the slaves to not rebel but wait for the accumulated goodness of their slave master to bring some small benefits.

"The true triumph", Slavoj Žižek says (2014, 180), "is not victory over the enemy; it occurs when the enemy itself starts to use your language, so that your ideas form the foundation of the entire field." But that is also a time to be vigilant and to not let mere words deceive.

2

From Absurd to Ethical:
What is Philanthropic Capitalism?

In the spring of 2010 four Danish youths started an enterprise called 'Initiative for Life' where one can buy a student's cap. The proceeds go to educate Ethiopian children, and on their website www.initiativforliv.dk they write: "When you buy Initiative for Life's cap you not only get a good price but also a good conscience." The project is supported by Save the Children, and what is of interest here is the blending of sales and charity, the good price and the good conscience. This is but one small example of a contemporary trend to de-differentiate capitalism and charity, increasingly summarized under the label philanthropic capitalism.

Philanthropic capitalism is the idea that *capitalism is or can be charitable in and of itself*. The claim is that capitalist mechanisms are superior to all others (especially the state) when it comes to not only creating economic but also human progress; that the market and market actors are or should be made the prime creators of the good society; that capitalism is not the problem but the solution to all the major problems in the world; that the best thing to do is to extend the market to hitherto private or state processes; and, finally, that there is no conflict between the rich and the poor, but that the rich is rather the poor's best and possibly only friend.

This is why Slavoj Žižek quite provocatively talks of the "liberal communists of Porto Davos", that is a fusion of capitalists and left-wing radicals, a fusion of the summits in Davos and Porto Alegre which are different but represent not so different expressions and celebrations of a new post-national, post-bureaucratic, post-state constellation which they both think usher in a new 'smart' era where smart "means dynamic and nomadic against centralized bureaucracy; dialogue and cooperation against central authority; flexibility against routine; culture and knowledge against old industrial production; and spontaneous interaction against fixed hierarchy." (Žižek 2006)

One can interpret philanthropic capitalism as the latest version of the modern era anti-revolutionary, pro-capitalist claims that a rebellion against capitalism will only end in misery and that there is actually no opposition between the market and the good. In the 1990s, the dominant versions of this anti-revolutionary claim were Francis Fukuyama's thesis of liberal-democratic capitalism as the last good idea and the hype of a high-tech, net-based 'crisis free' economy (Frank 2000). Both claims quickly lost persuasive force. The IT-bubble crashed at the beginning of 2000 and the movement critical of globalization seriously questioned whether the 'G8 World Order' was the only world possible. It seems, therefore, fair to interpret the enormous attention to and hope in philanthropic capitalism as an attempt to close the deficit of legitimacy of contemporary 'flexible capitalism' where some get ever more but even more get so much less; a development not halted but rather accelerated by the 2008 financial crisis.

The purpose of this small book is to analyze the contemporary version of the interrelations between present day philanthropy and a new form of so-called 'creative' or 'flexible' capitalism. My claim is basically that philanthropic capitalism is a sub-form of a new flexible capitalism in practical terms and even more forcefully legitimating in its intent. We should then not understand it as a mere appendix to or insignificant advertising trick of capitalism but rather as a fully integrated part of the way in which capitalism is operating and legitimating itself at present (Žižek 2009, chap. 1; Nielsen 2009).

The main theoretical inspiration is from Luc Boltanski and Ève Chiapello and their *The new spirit of capitalism* (Boltanski & Chiapello 2005), from which I will interpret philanthropic capitalism as an answer to a critique, or rather as a way to integrate the critique into the self-portrayal of capitalism. We have, for instance, seen capitalist firms turning the critique of being inauthentic into a 'self-critical' maneuver using a vocabulary of a new playful, ironic, creative, leveling corporate culture to distance themselves from their own inauthentic past (Frank 1997). An ideology or spirit is basically a self-representation developed and conceptualized through an active engagement with the structural features of the economy and with societal pressures and critiques.

Capitalism needs such a spirit in order to appear legitimate. Repeating an idea from Max Weber, Boltanski and Chiapello state that "capitalism is an absurd system" (Boltanski & Chiapello 2005, 7) meaning that it doesn't provide its own legitimacy but needs to find it in the outside world and that it needs such a legitimating spirit in order to justify engagement in capitalist practices. This means that a capitalist spirit serves legitimating purposes for everyone. It provides explanations for the entrepreneur working day and night to start a new company, for the worker clocking in and out, for the manager supervising or firing a workforce, for the day-trader frantically buying and selling, for politicians legislating (or not) on economic practices etc. Boltanski and Chiapello say:

> *The spirit of capitalism is precisely the set of beliefs associated with the capitalist order that helps justify this order and, by legitimating them, to sustain the forms of action and predispositions compatible with it. These justifications, whether general or practical, local or global, expressed in terms of virtue or justice, support the performance of more or less unpleasant tasks and, more generally, adhesion to a lifestyle conducive to the capitalist order. In this instance, we may indeed speak of a dominant ideology, so long as we stop regarding it as a mere subterfuge by the dominant to ensure the consent of the dominated, and acknowledge that a majority of those*

involved – the strong as well as the weak – rely on these schemas in order to represent to themselves the operation, benefits and constraints of the order in which they find themselves immersed. (Ibid., 10-11)

They investigate "the way in which the ideologies associated with economic activity are altered" (Ibid., 3) and they identify historically grounded ideologies or spirits that are basically the way in which capitalism presents itself, the ways in which it asks to be evaluated, the ways in which it enables but also constrains its practice. I will argue that philanthropy is one of the ideological elements in the new spirit of capitalism, a capitalism integrating ethical, emotional, relational, cognitive and now also ecological resources into the heart of all capitalist processes (Chiapello 2013). Philanthropic capitalism is the element in the new spirit of capitalism that is most aggressively integrating the ethical critique of capitalism into an asset.

Of interest here is the ideological function that philanthropic capitalism shares with other recent phenomena like 'green accounts', 'corporate social responsibility', and the like, seeking with new concepts and arguments to repeat what the president of General Motors allegedly said in 1953: 'What is good for General Motors is good for America and vice versa'. Philanthropic capitalism is the claim that what is good for the rich is good for the poor and vice versa. This book will not address the question of philanthropy's effects but only philanthropic capitalism as a symptom and sign of contemporary capitalism and its alleged deficit of legitimacy.

Philanthropy has always been dependent upon inequality and hierarchy. Inequality is the reason why philanthropy is needed and the riches of the more fortunate are what provide the material for philanthropy. Therefore, inequality is both the reason and the resources of philanthropy. But inequality takes on many forms. It is dependent upon the economy in which it exists, just as are the legitimating narratives of inequality (Wilkinson & Pickett 2010). At present, we seem to be witnessing, despite the financial crisis, the deepening of an 'entrepreneurial', 'creative', or 'flexible' capitalism offering huge opportunities for some and condemning still more to increasingly precarious forms of existence (OECD 2011, 2014). One of the main claims in this book is that present philanthropic practices, and more importantly the conceptualization of philanthropy, has much to do with a new form of global capitalism systematically dividing up the risks and the rewards (Harvey 2005, 2010; Crouch 2011, chap. 1+2).

In his remarkable book, *Debt – the first 5,000 years*, anthropologist David Graeber discusses hierarchy as a counterpart to exchange, the latter implying formal equality.

In contrast, relations of explicit hierarchy – that is, relations between at least two parties in which one is considered superior to the other – do not tend to operate by reciprocity at all. It's hard to see because the relation is often justified in reciprocal terms ('the peasants provide food, the lords provide protection'), but the principle by which they operate is exactly the opposite. (Graeber 2011, 109)

Charity is dependent upon non-reciprocity. Just imagine what would happen if a recipient of aid gave back the same or a larger amount to the initial giver. Then, Graeber presents a "continuum of one-sided social relations, ranging from the most exploitative to the most benevolent. At one extreme is theft, or plunder; on the other selfless charity." (Ibid.). What this tells us is, that just as with inequality, charity may be generous and selfless but it is dependent upon and is reproducing hierarchy. It is, Graeber says, only at the two extremes that one can have interactions with complete strangers. Anonymous giving has a long tradition where both the giver and the receiver remain unidentified to each other. However, as all charity organizations pragmatically know, there needs to be a face (preferably a child or a woman) on the recipient and also a naming or self-branding opportunity for the giver. This apparent discrepancy between anonymity and identification and its moral implications is not my issue. It is rather the hierarchy inherent in philanthropy and why 'it's hard to see', as Graeber wrote in the quote hereinabove. That is, how inequality tends to 'hide' behind a new charity discourse of intense emotional and monetary investment by the givers for the recipients of the charity.

What may be an indication of something new in contemporary philanthropy is exactly this emotional disposition on the part of the giver, this refusal to keep the recipient a stranger, the need to familiarize oneself with the one in need. Personal commitment (real or simulated) is the new entry point of the giver just as empowerment is the new supposed exit point of the recipient. In the following, I will explore what this change in philanthropy tells us about our present social and economic condition. The aim is purely diagnostic, being sort of a situation report of the interlocked changes of both philanthropy and capitalism, and one should not expect any prognostic or prescriptive conclusions.

3

Capital Selves:
Competition and Inequality

Inequality and climate change are capitalism's two most fateful legitimating challenges. In her recent book, Naomi Klein (2014) has persuasively shown how climate change denial and climate change profiting are two sides of the same neoliberal coin. On a vastly smaller scale, this book tries to do the same with inequality, claiming that the celebration of inequality as the road to prosperity – the classical free market chant – and the new philanthropic capitalist voices concerned with inequality's dire effects on the world's populations and societies, are really not two positions but one and pro-inequality at that.

It is easy to get morally outraged by comments like this one from American free market enthusiast Dennis Gartman:

We celebrate income disparity and we applaud the growing margins between the bottom 20% of American society and the upper 20% for it is evidence of what has made America a great country. It is the chance to have a huge income ... to make something of one's self; to begin a business and become a millionaire legally and on one's own that separates the US from most other nations of the world. Do we feel bad for the growing gap between the rich and the poor in the US? Of course not; we celebrate it, for we were poor once and we are reasonably wealthy now. We did it on our own, by the sheer dint of will, tenacity, street smarts and the like. That is why immigrants come to the US: to join the disparate income earners at the upper levels of society and to leave poverty behind. Income inequality? Give us a break? God bless income disparity and those who have succeeded, and shame upon the OWS crowd who take us to task for our success and wallow in their own failure. Income disparity? Feh!

What we despise is government that imposes rules that prohibit or make it difficult to make even more money; to employ even more people; to give even more sums to the charities of our choice. That is what we despise. (quoted by Hume 2011)

How should one respond however, when Barack Obama, Bill Gates, the Pope, and most everyone else names inequality the great economic and moral challenge of our times? Some of the clues are in the Gartman quote, and we will revisit the ideas of entrepreneurial "will, tenacity, street smarts" throughout the book, but for now let's just notice the latter part where he speaks of despising a "government that imposes rules that prohibit or make it difficult to make even more money", on the one hand, and the idea that freeing capitalism of regulatory control will allow people like him "to give even more sums to the charities of our choice." Neoliberalism and a sense of entitlement go together, or rather: neoliberalism is the legitimating narrative of why some are richer than others. But to understand its appeal way beyond the ranks of the 1% and their heavily subsidized hordes of talking minions, and to see how neoliberalism can both celebrate and bemoan inequality, we need to take a quick tour into neoliberalism itself.

Through the 1970s a critique of state and bureaucracy developed. A marked sense of multiple crises matured into a massive devaluation of centralized authorities of all kinds, public and private. The 'ossified' structures of the old society were to give way to a new liberation. On the right, this was phrased in terms of a rediscovery of *the market*, or rather as 'more choice', 'free choice', and 'freedom to choose' actualized as deregulation, privatization, liberalization, in a word: corporatization and later by the introduction of market-like conditions in the public sector (Rodgers 2011, 41-76). On the left, the new times were coined through the language of *civil society* summed up in 'more participation' and 'true democracy' actualized through local democracy, council systems and the decentralization of the public sector. Both left and right connected their critiques and programs to a revaluation of *the self*, spoken of as 'more self-determination', 'freedom', 'autonomy', and a bit later 'creativity' and 'self-management'. These different discourses addressed some of the same issues, were part of a parallel anti-bureaucratic consensus and liberal phraseology, and divided the social world into concepts and imagery of the flow versus the static.

This helps explain the multidimensionality of the concept of flexibility, which is so important to understand for a true grasp of the seductive powers of neoliberalism. From the 1970s onwards, a new conceptualization of flexibility developed, one positing opportunity versus rigidity, that is, an individualization of flexibility as making oneself current and relevant continuously. Flexibility comes to mean potential for the future, and its counterpart are obstacles of human action. What used to be described as stability or security gets rebranded as "unfreedom". We can begin to grasp neoliberalism as more than an economic program when we see how the individual is described through the language of potentiality rather than vulnerability, through the language of liberation rather than satisfaction, the responsible and active rather than the needy and other-relying, the endless rather than the limited.

The reconstructive languages of the market, civil society and self-served, for all their conflicts in establishing a difference between the individual and 'the system', with that difference opening up a conceptual and cognitive void filled by a market rhetoric of flexibility and entrepreneurialism, are three expressions of the same market conditioning system of an uncertain future that we confront alone. The flexible adapts to the ever-changing conditions, and the entrepreneur endlessly recreates the conditions. What that means is that the "character of the entrepreneur is no longer represented as one among many ethical personalities but assumes ontological priority" (du Gay

1994, 662; Keat & Abercrombie 1991; Heelas & Morris 1992), with 'the flexible' being the adapted version for all the not quite so daring of us, and measured according to the entrepreneurial standard. Decoupling from communities and securities is described as liberation, of being one's own master, of being a true self (coupled with self-righteous intolerance toward the lazy, the irresponsible, the unproductive, the welfare slaves). However false, the seductive powers of neoliberalism consist of this vision of entrepreneurial selves for everyone. More than anything else it is the generalization of the entrepreneur that is behind both the success and the "strange non-death of neoliberalism." (Crouch 2011; Frank 2012). And nothing teaches entrepreneurialism to a public more than the many different market invocations of *flexibility as freedom*.

Unlike the neoliberalism of pre-WW2, which advocated laissez-faire and a major retrenchment of the state, the neoliberalism developed after the war and that came to power and prominence from the 1970s onwards, argues for a radical restructuring of state and people. The classical neoliberalism had a static, zero-sum view of the state and market where one could only grow at the expense of the other and where their basic principles remained unchangeable. The new neoliberalism sported a dynamic view of both. Starting with economic competition as a master narrative, the neoliberalism we know today started viewing and using the state to create a generalized competition between and within all social units from the state to the individual itself. One of its architects, Milton Friedman explained in 1951 the difference between new and old neoliberalism:

Neo-liberalism would accept the nineteenth century liberal emphasis on the fundamental importance of the individual, but it would substitute for the nineteenth century goal of laissez-faire as a means to this end, the goal of the competitive order. It would seek to use competition among producers to protect consumers from exploitation, competition among employers to protect workers and owners of property, and competition among consumers to protect the enterprises themselves. The state would police the system, establish conditions favorable to competition and prevent monopoly, provide a stable monetary framework, and relieve acute misery and distress. The citizens would be protected against the state by the existence of a free private market; and against one another by the preservation of competition. (Friedman 1951)

In clear opposition to the classical neoliberalism, the new doesn't really care if everything *is* a market as long as everyone behaves *as* on a market, or as Michel Foucault stated: "Basically, [the neoliberal government] has to intervene in society so that competitive mechanisms can play a regulatory role at every moment and every point in society and by intervening in this way its objective will become possible, that is to say, a general regulation of society by the market." (Foucault 2008, 145). It is not that contemporary neoliberals don't favor privatizations and liberalizations – or corporatizations as they should properly be called – but we should not look singly or primarily for the effects of neoliberalism in the retrenchment of the state but also, or rather, in its restructuring as part of the competitive order. Maybe *competition* is the proper term for the restructuring of the state, for the neoliberal state, and for the new subject; the creation of competitive logics where other principles used to reign (social justice, solidarity, communality, sacrifice …). Described by Jamie Peck (2010, xii) as "politically assisted market rule", neo-liberalization is the attempt to impose the market model on any social organization of collective or private life. The state and the individual gets reformatted as competitive units, in competition with other units – globalization as the master narrative for them both – and amongst themselves. The state along with its offices and departments are divided into 'self-governing' units competing with each other, legitimized by fiscal restraints, global competition, and the idea that only life-and-death-competition makes you creative, adaptive, and flexible. The individual is re-described in capital terms. 'Entrepreneur of self' is the generalized individual as capital, investing in him- or herself, constantly optimizing, moving, learning, in a word: innovating. One is not only in competition with others but with oneself, where the self is as opposed to the self needed in the near but uncertain future. A constant temporal splitting of the self is installed, forever threatening with the prospect of one's self becoming obsolete, unmarketable, dead capital.

Once re-described as capital, one has individuals portrayed as potentiality either lying dormant and uncirculating, or invested and circulating. The role of the state comes to ensure the free circulation of capital – in all its forms. This helps explain Gartman's comments about a "government that imposes rules that prohibit or make it difficult to make even more money". That is more than rich talk. It is a message of the liberation of humankind, it is freedom realized in man's opposition to the state, to bureaucracy, to blocked or regulated circulation. It's freedom as flow. It's freedom as competition, and as William Davies notes in his recent book on neoliberalism: "To argue in favor of competition and competitiveness is necessarily to argue in favour of inequality, given that competitive activity is defined partly by the fact that it pursues an unequal outcome. Processes and rules which facilitate (or aim to facilitate) competition can themselves be understood as offering a normative sanction for inequality in some way." (Davies 2014, 37).

What we are going to observe throughout this book is that philanthropic capitalism is all about the marketization and competition of the social, about using the market and capital as the master principles for pushing neoliberalization into areas where other forces – state welfare, charity and solidarity – used to operate. The reason this can work legitimatly is because competition subscribes to both equality and inequality. It seductively proclaims a level playing field, invites people to the field, calls them real and able players – in this case through philanthropic capitalist activities – and pretends that the game is fair for all. In the words of Davies (Ibid., 41), "competition represents a paradoxical combination of equality and inequality. The structure of an organized competition (including in the liberal imaginary, a market) involves contestants being *formally equal at the outset and empirically unequal at the conclusion."*

4

Charity Button:
Consumer Philanthropy

In Danish supermarkets, one can press the 'charity button' and donate the bottle refund money to sick children rather than get it for themselves. Increasingly, we see philanthropy being embedded in everyday consumption. There are products that are themselves charitable: ecological or fair trade products, but we also see that the purchase of other products is given an extra-moral dimension that is not related to the actual product but derived from its purchase. The company behind the product promises to give a share of the price to some charitable cause thereby linking consumption and charity.

Ecology, fair trade and consumer philanthropy are all expressions of political consumption but should also be understood within the framework of what 'the new spirit of capitalism' promises to produce, namely an emotional and moral dimension to purely economic activity. By buying these 'philanthro-capitalist products', you get in a sense more than you pay for. You get the product and its utility value, but you also get to do good. There is an added dimension to the purchase that mirrors a larger trend in contemporary capitalism. The immediate output is no longer enough. Pay is no longer enough reward for one's work. There has to be personal growth as well. The product is no longer enough. There has to be an added dimension of experience, meaning, or morality along with the consumption or purchase. The logic of 'Get two, pay for one' is no longer reserved for the quantitative part of shopping but is now also applicable in its qualitative part, in what we can call the moral surplus value of shopping.

This moral surplus value is embedded in the shopping

situation itself, in the heart of the basic market relation of buying and selling. Charity is here directly and positively correlated with private consumption. The more you purchase, the more good you do. To choose this product rather than that, to click the charity button rather than get the money for yourself is doubly charitable. It is charitable for the ones getting the money but also for the one doing the shopping or clicking. Consumer philanthropy is therefore, the individual-psychological component in the ideological complex that claims that there is today no opposition between consumption (enjoyment) and charity (morality), just as the work-organizational logic says that there is no opposition between work as pay and work as individual growth. Both are indicative of a shift in the promise made by capitalism going from the scarcity society's promise of welfare through the state, to the post-scarcity society's promise of liberation and morality in and through capitalism itself.

While politicized consumption has been known for a very long time in the struggles of workers, women, ethnic minorities and others, the prevalent tendency today is to have individualized 'political' consumption without any social movement component. The philanthropic consumer is distinguished from the political consumer by the development of "the individual who is imagined and acted upon by the imperative to consume" (Miller & Rose 2008, 114; Bauman 2005, chap. 2; Payne 2012; Olsen forthcoming), by the neoliberal construction of the 'sovereign consumer' who is imagined to be wholly free to purchase what they please; who can purchase anything from anywhere; who gains his or her main pleasure from shopping; who is never bound or restricted by past consumptions; who never stops shopping. The sovereign consumer is one of the contemporary personifications of capital, that is, a reframing of the individual in capital terms. The sovereign consumer is the one whose full spectrum of desires and wishes are fulfilled through consumption, whose passion economy is actualized through the economy, with philanthropic consumption being the means to achieve moral fulfilment in consumptive practice.

At my local supermarket, one places small plastic barriers between the groceries on the cash register belt. Mostly printed advertisements are printed on them, but some of them have the imprint: 'You too can give to charity. Donate your refund to sick children'. The problem is that once you're standing in line and placing your groceries on the cash register belt, it is too late to press the charity button for your change, so what it does is only to stimulate bad consciousness when standing there with your receipt. Taking a cue from Campbell Jones' wonderful notion of "the subject supposed to recycle" (Jones 2010), this is the articulation of the subject supposed to donate. The possibility and the free choice to give the money turns out to be really a moral imperative: We are supposed to in the strong sense, and that we should and, moreover, must, and not do so, would make us guilty of a breach. "So", Oprah Winfrey said in a TV charity show, "by just buying a t-shirt, a pair of jeans, even a cell phone, you can actually begin to save lives." (quoted from Richey & Ponte 2011, 2-3; on Oprah Winfrey as a neoliberal icon see Peck 2008). To choose not to recycle or donate or consume (!) "is an act of bad faith, a careless failure of duty, responsibility and care." (Jones 2010, 30). That breach and the guilt associated with it are also what are invoked in standing there with your groceries.

The button at the refund machine is not really there for you to choose. The option of getting the money is only really there to simulate an option, but it is an all-important simulation because the creation of a 'choice situation' is what gives the donation its moral character and its emotional enjoyment. It is in this case not consumption but rather the abstention from consumption that is the enjoyment, but it comes out of a very special subjectivation passing off choice as duty. And it obligates us to ask "where the image of the subject supposed to recycle [and donate] comes from" (Ibid., 37) and to notice that this subjectivation is part of a larger trend to shift agency onto individual subjects (as we shall see below) and away from economic and political power, as well as from all of us not as individuals (consumers, donators) but as citizens. Why is ecology, animal welfare, proper working conditions, fair prices and individual choice something we can choose or not? What is that ominous de-politicization of issues that could be decided collectively?

Consumer philanthropy, like the others detailed below, is dependent upon a particular focus on the individual. Collective or institutional effort is consistently downgraded in favor of individual engagement and personal motivation. This is evident in former US president Bill Clinton's book *Giving – how each of us can change the world* which is basically a catalogue of outstanding individuals making a difference. Even when the topic is government, the focus is on individuals giving. Running through the book is a special way of addressing the reader: "Most of us aren't public figures like Mia Farrow, Don Cheadle, or George Clooney who can use their fame to do good, but each of us has the ability to do something." (Clinton 2007, 203). And, Clinton reminds us, "if everyone did it, we would change the world." (Ibid., 55). This is change coming out of individual choices of consumption or donation rather than common action. Therefore, although Clinton is – now, as an ex-president – a fair defender of public responsibilities, his narrative fits in with a depoliticized, ethical subjectivation turning the commitment inwards rather than the effort outwards.

The bottle water company Thirsty Planet has a slogan called 'Buy a bottle. Change a life!' Vinicius Brei and Steffen Böhm, who have analyzed the CSR-strategies of 'ethical' bottled water, wherefrom the slogan is taken, emphasize that these consumer philanthropic "campaigns are always emotional and persuasive, trying to closely connect the bottled water consumer to the African problem of lack of water. The campaigns urge consumers to 'get involved' and 'participate' in solving this problem by buying a bottle of branded water." (Brei & Böhm 2011, 244)

Involvement, participation and compassion are translated into consumption. The difference one can make, so these campaigns tell us, is through buying stuff. The ethical dilemma of our abundance (here of water) and of others lack thereof is paradoxically solved through us consuming more. Inequality becomes the solution rather than being the problem.

Here, we may briefly invoke Hannah Arendt's critique of the politicization of private emotions in *On revolution*. Political compassion is solidarity, which establishes "a community of interest with the oppressed and exploited". It "partakes of reason and hence generality" (Arendt 1965, 88), whereas pity is the emotional or perverse side of compassion where the emotional attachment of the private sphere is superimposed upon strangers suffering. What Arendt seems to be saying is that one can either acknowledge the human in the one suffering or one can, through pity, enact a familiarity that imitates the suffering stranger as one's friend, hence depoliticizing but also emotionally intensifying the relation. Is that not what contemporary expressions of philanthropy do when they insistently mimic a relation, a 'partnership', between blatant unequals? The suffering other and the consuming self is what gets celebrated in contemporary consumer philanthropy (Giroux 1994, chap. 1). What pity enables is to invest emotionally in the suffering other; imitating the help one gives a friend, while keeping that other at a comfortable distance from oneself.

This is emotional response without cost, caring at a distance, resulting in an acute depoliticization of the reasons for the suffering. What philanthropic capitalism is portraying is ideal victims (Christie 1986) – or rather ideal sufferers – whose story (and purpose) is one of suffering, not of repression or injustice. In their critique of the RED campaign, where a certain percentage of money earned from products with the RED label are given to charity, Lisa Ann Richey and Stefano Ponte draw our attention to the glittery and person fixated representation of the Western celebrities promoting the campaign, as well as the enjoyment of the Western consumer purchasing the RED products – "You can feel great about spending, whether you are buying cappuccinos or cashmere", as the RED American Express campaign says, giving their take on the African AIDS pandemic: "Has there ever been a better reason to shop?" (quoted from Richey & Ponte 2011, xi) These personal stories and enjoyments are contrasted with the images of the African, often nameless, bare life – the subject supposed to suffer – "counted in the calculation of 'lives saved' as easily as pill counts or merchandise inventory. Africans with AIDS are presented in smooth, virtual representations in which 'global politics' is reduced to style." (Ibid., xii; Farell 2012)

This kind of activity inevitably makes a connection between charity and your pleasure, and between charity and consumption, two connections in which genuine progress may easily lose out when it's a choice of deciding between sweaters as to which charity gets (a fraction of) your money, or because other important things like third world labor practices or environmental impacts are not visible in the 'buy two and save an African'-consumption advertising. Are people really suffering and dying of preventable diseases because affluent Westerners have failed to consume enough products? Is the environment, and the climate most of all, best served by 'smarter' consumption or less? In a spoof on the RED-campaign there is truth in the slogan of the webpage www.buylesscrap.org: "Shopping is not a solution. Buy (Less). Give More." (Waal 2008, 48)

Consumer philanthropy turns the citizen into a consumer. In the words of the RED-campaign, it is "the consumer battalion gathering in the shopping malls." (quoted in Rimmer 2010, 317). You buy, they live. But this is precisely no battalion, movement or mobilization. It is an individualization and privatization of our common duty; it is the sacrifice sometimes needed to help others turned into a hedonistic delight; it is the lie that we can all win, they their lives, and I a new t-shirt. It is learning that we can continue our way of life untroubled. The climate and the poor will be served and saved by our individual consumption choices; not by tedious and costly political action or consumption sacrifices, but by buying smart and buying more.

5

'Doing Good while Doing Great':
Corporate Philanthropy

In an article entitled "What's Wrong with Profit?", Alan Abramson, director of the nonprofit sector and philanthropy program at the Aspen Institute is quoted as saying: "More and more people are asking who else is going to finance doing good if government isn't." Speaking of corporate leaders he continues: "These guys have firsthand knowledge of the market's power, and they're asking themselves why they can't make money and tackle some of the problems once addressed primarily by government at the same time." (Strom 2006). This sentiment was echoed by Kurt Hoffmann, director of Shell Foundation, who said: "Charities have failed for decades to deliver [...] do we continue with the status quo or apply some fresh, inherently effective and potentially very effective thinking to find new solutions?" (quoted in Edwards 2010, 3) The presumption made of two separate camps consisting of state or NGO efforts, thought to be ineffective and static, and the business community thought to be inherently (!) effective, is the cornerstone of corporate philanthropy ideology.

Traditionally, businesses have thought of philanthropy as something to be done after office hours and with the profits earned, and then most often as basically a PR-thing. The trend right now is to think of philanthropy as part of competitiveness planning (Porter & Kramer 2002; Johansen 2010) but also of the capitalist enterprise as philanthropic in and of itself (Smith 1994; Byrne 2002). The thinking is summarized in the title of Curt Weeden's book on philanthropy, *Smart giving is good business* with the telling subtitle *How corporate philanthropy can benefit your company and society* (Weeden 2011) and in various consulting initiatives like http://measuringphilanthropy.com/ helping corporations to give profitably. Manifesting itself here is the claim of an indistinction between company interest and societal interest, and even more fundamentally, between profit-making and doing good. Or as the founder of Oracle, Larry Ellison, has said: "The profit motive may be the best tool for solving the world's problems, more effective than any government or private philanthropy." (quoted from Edwards 2008, 12)

Corporate philanthropy is the idea that private capitalism and its business model provides the solution to a whole range of societal and global problems; that these solutions are superior to all alternatives, especially state and private philanthropy; and that the solutions come about not as a result of using the surplus from capitalist profit-making but rather from using capitalism, and especially the profit-model, as the means themselves. This connects to the new forms of value creation that "derives not only from the production of goods and services that extract surplus value from the labor process, but the manipulation of images that convince consumers of the firm's integrity." (Fleming 2009, 3) Corporate philanthropy is part of the turn to authenticity in seemingly all spheres of life, including corporate life, stating that business and profit – just like work for the laborer – is not really the goal but just the means to something else and better.

Bill Gates, who is one of the most generous and prominent philanthropists, has summarized the rationale behind corporate philanthropy in a 2008-article on creative capitalism. He acknowledges the efforts from governmental and non-profit groups:

> [...] but it will take too long if they try to do it alone. It is mainly corporations that have the skills to make technological innovations work for the poor. To make most of those skills we need a more creative capitalism: an attempt to stretch the reach of market forces so that more companies can benefit from doing work that makes people better off. We need new ways to bring far more people into the

system – capitalism – that has done so much good in the world. (Gates 2008)

The ruling idea – or rather ideology – behind this is that businesses, qua the profit motive, are organized rationally and pragmatically unlike the political and private charity organizations ruled by ideological prejudices and vested interests. The ideology of the smart business however, is disproved every day (Cassidy 2010; Smith 2012). Businesses are no more rational, efficient or effective than any other social organization. Read any newspaper, work in any business. There is no inherent superiority in their business model, but there is exuberant confidence in the model, a confidence that has infected politicians, civil servants, NGOs, and the media.

Corporate philanthropy is heavily dependent upon an impatient technical fix-approach to the world and a near-total dismissal of 'traditional politics' as a way to solve problems, evident most clearly in Google's engineer approach to philanthropy (Strom & Helft 2011). Kasper Kofod, partner in the design company Social Action, coupling businesses and charities, expresses it thus:

The politicians do theirs but it just takes such long time. The political machine is a giant fleet to get going. That is why I would never go into politics to make a difference. The corporate world is more dynamic than political life. Politicians are simply not good enough to give their own citizens the tools they need to give direct assistance. Corporations can do that. (quoted from Lavrsen 2008)

The consensus on devaluing politics and the state runs through all this literature. It is presented not as a historically contingent process initiated and radicalized by neoliberalism and globalism but as an obvious fact outside any human control. The chairman of the World Economic Forum held annually at Davos, Klaus

Schwab, wrote an article in 2008 about global corporate citizenship. While much could be said about the significant elevation of the corporation into a citizen, what is more pertinent here is how the 'decline of the state' is depoliticized to make room for the corporation to step in and fill the gap. "Today's corporate engagement in society is the *inevitable* result of a number of factors. First, the role of the nation-state has diminished." (Schwab 2008, 108). Not a word is uttered of the political decisions of delimiting and privatizing state functions, of the decisions to globalize economies, finance especially, and to allocate decision power to corporate rather than political levels. It is solely described as the result of nature-like developments called 'globalization' and 'advances in technology'. This lack of analytical finesse allows for the conclusion: "As state power has shrunk, the sphere of influence of business has widened." (Ibid., 109). Like a vacuum being filled, the ahistorical, apolitical narrative positions corporations as "integral to the survival of governments and the political stability of nations and regions." (Ibid.). What is missing from this narrative, obviously, is any understanding of the role of corporations and capital in disinvesting the state, of corporate takeover of state functions, of global tax avoidance and other activities, jeopardizing the state. The cure from this is then more corporate dominance. That is not philanthropy, but privatization, a universalization of the business model to solve problems, at least in part, created by corporations.

Businesses, the argument goes, are tuned into getting a 'return on their investment'. Only businesses are able to respond quickly, efficiently, and responsively to philanthropic needs because that is what they do in relation to all their customers. It is not only the profit and business model being universalized but also the customer type as the general human. People in need are just like customers: identify the need, provide its satisfaction. This connects very precisely to the market value of appropriating social life and ethical demands, namely a way to get into the welfare market that the state is retreating from and is actively seeking both market and civil society replacements for. Shedding its pure market profile for a caring one is one way to approach the 'market' of welfare. It is what Gerard Hanlon and Peter Fleming very precisely call a "soft power form of extending corporate influence" and it emerged to "fill the legitimation breech left in wake of a reconfigured state." (Hanlon & Fleming 2009, 939, 942; see also Hanlon 2008). A simultaneous upsurge in ethical demands and abandonment of the state (receiving its first ideological name as Tony Blair's Third Way) is both verbalized and responded to by corporations today.

Corporate philanthropy is then to be understood as a sub-category of Corporate Social Responsibility, meaning an active embrace of social responsibilities by companies. Ronen Shamir identifies an all-important element in this when he says that "corporations have assertively embarked on the Social Responsibility bandwagon, gradually shaping the very notion of Social Responsibility in ways amenable to corporate concerns." (Shamir 2004, 675-6). Like all the other examples given in this book, CSR is, among other things, also a way to answer the ethical demand in a way that doesn't hinder but rather promotes capitalist processes. "The new formula", Giorgio Armani said when launching his RED Emporio Armani product line at the summit at Davos, "is that this is charity to the world of course, but particularly it is the fact that commerce will no longer have a negative connotation." (quoted from Richey & Ponte 2011, 5)

It may often be a PR-way to deflect criticism, a 'self-regulation' of responsibilities, as Shamir names it, to avoid legislatively imposed responsibilities. It is certainly a way to maintain control in a corporate environment of 'ethical consumers', 'creative employees', 'critical publics', 'investigative media' and 'activist mobilization'. Embedding CSR into corporate culture (real or fake) is a way of answering a critique through self-promoting the standards that one wants to be measured upon, knowing that other and possibly stricter standards of good behavior are out there gaining momentum. CSR is, ideologically speaking, a way to answer criticism while looking "to be governed by good will alone" (Shamir 2004, 677; Utting 2005), that is by one's own altruistic motives.

Businesses may well be good at producing stuff but it is absurd to think that social complexity is reducible to supply and demand. As Michael Edwards pointedly says:

> [T]here's no vaccine against greed, fear, poverty, inequality, corruption, lousy governance, personal alienation, and all the other things that plague us. Few areas of business expertise translate well into the very different world of complex social and political problems, where solutions have to be fought for and negotiated – not produced, packaged, and sold. (Edwards 2010, 8)

The ideological trickery of corporate philanthropy is to present the market model as the general model and any other as inefficient, wasteful, all talk, bureaucratic etc. Not recognizing the efforts and purposes of others is a good way not to acknowledge their worth. Giving the word once more to Edwards:

> After all, if business wants to save the world, there are plenty of opportunities to do so at the heart of their operations: pay your taxes as a good corporate citizen; don't produce goods that kill, exploit, or maim people; pay decent wages and provide benefits to your workers; don't subvert politics to pursue your short-term interests; obey the regulations that govern markets in the public interest; and stop creating monopolies and other market manipulations so that other firms can prosper and wealth can be more widely shared. (Ibid., 31)

In other words, don't come to us with all the good you want to do in the world. Clean up your own act and push the rest of the business community to do the same. Then we can talk.

6

Think like a Corporation!
The Charitable Industrial Complex

In a discussion of the Gates foundation and the notion of creative capitalism, a writer for the *Financial Times* said: "This is bringing business ideas to philanthropy, not bringing philanthropic ideas to business." (Crook 2009, 113). A prominent element in corporate philanthropy is a sort of reversed CSR, which we could call philanthro-business or, as Peter Buffett, son of Warren Buffett and a dedicated philanthropist himself, has called it, "the charitable-industrial complex." (Buffett 2013; a piece heavily attacked on http://philanthrocapitalism.net/). The issue is not a humanization of the corporation but rather a marketization of philanthropy (Weisberg 2006; Foster 2007), neatly summarized by Bill Clinton: "The same strategies businesses use to organize and expand markets that enhance the public good and empower their customers to do the same [!] can be adopted by nongovernmental organizations involved in philanthropic work." (Clinton 2007, 178; see also Hoffman 2008 & Prahalad 2005)

The main impetus behind this transformation seems to be a response similar to the companies, namely a response to critiques for being in this case wasteful, ineffective, and overly bureaucratic. This critique is part of the stated rationale behind philanthropic capitalist initiatives but is also the driving force behind the marketization of aid organizations, with the market and business being the reigning models for organizational design today.

The market approach to philanthropy tells you to look at philanthropic needs as you would any other need on a market, and on doners as you would any other customer. As a member of Google's charity fund, Sheryl Sandberg, has said: "We look at the most efficient ways to solve the world's problems" (quoted from Lee 2006) – and that is increasingly the way of the market. Witness the 2003 UN Global Compact report *The 21st Century NGO: In the Market for Change* illustrated on the front page with shopping trolleys and inside with consumer market pictures plastered over with posters screaming 'change'. Their recommendation to the NGOs reads: "The first thing is to recognize that markets are central to [NGO's] future. Markets are becoming legitimate channels for social change – and are also likely to be, on balance, more efficient and effective than many traditional approaches." (UN Global Compact 2003, 3; Hopgood 2008). This is why philanthropy has to copy the methods and organizational designs of capitalism and private business to develop what an American center calls 'effective philanthropy' (on 'effective' in contemporary philanthropy see Katz 2005). The center "provides foundations and other philanthropic funders with comparative data to enable higher performance" and on its website (www.effectivephilanthropy.org) lists the core parameters of effective philanthropy as:

- Assessing Performance
  - How are we doing? How do we know?
- Developing Strategy
  - Is our strategy clear, coherent, and well-implemented?
- Optimizing Governance
  - Is our board engaged and effective?
- Funder-Grantee Relationships
  - Are we working productively with our grantees?
- Managing Operations
  - Are our staff satisfied and high performing?

This universalization of business jargon is evident also at another such center, the British Impetus trust, which defines 'venture philanthropy' thus:

Venture philanthropy is an active approach to philanthropy, which involves giving skills as well as money. It uses the principles of venture capital, with the investee organisation receiving management support, specialist expertise and financial resources. The aim is for a social, rather than financial, return.
(http://www.impetus.org.uk/about-venture-philanthropy/)

One should, of course, notice here the little word 'active' discreetly shaming other philanthropic approaches. 'Venture philanthropists', 'upstart-charity', 'social investments', 'strategic philanthropy' and not least 'social entrepreneurs' are some of the terms in this growing indistinction between corporations and charities, both using a capitalist mindset, vocabulary and organization, and both seeing their job to provide good to 'philanthropic clients' (*The Economist* 2006; Deutsch 2006)

Philanthropic organizations increasingly compete for 'market shares'. They rent out their brand to corporations, solicit funds from private actors, shift from small membership donations to large corporate donations, invite business leaders onto their boards, sell merchandise, engage in financial trading and investment, restructure their organization along business models, compete for contracts, shift from volunteer work to increasingly well-paid professional managers and operatives etc. (Eikenberry & Kluver 2004). External market pressure and internal marketization develop in tandem. There is pressure forcing change but philanthropic organizations also to some extent push the development themselves by opting for a business evaluation model of their work and their organization. They have not defended their specificity but have basically agreed to evaluation standards coming from the market rather than civil society.

Fuelling philanthro-business is the conviction being retold repeatedly at present that the 'old methods' are obsolete and outdated. This is also what pushes corporate philanthropy onto center stage. The obsolete and outdated is state development aid and private 'unprofessional' charities. This is where they both tap into and deepen the ruling anti-bureaucratic consensus (du Gay 2000, chap. 3), showing how it is a critique with an in-built solution: private capitalism and the business model, as also evident in the contemporary development of welfare. This anti-bureaucratic consensus is mirrored by an equally prominent hope in management solutions; solutions always coming down to 'opening the flows', 'knocking down the bureaucracy', 'floating units', 'unleashing creativity', all "about replacing bureaucratic systems with entrepreneurial systems" as two of its prominent celebrators state (Osborne & Plastrik 1992, 14); and all of it is basically taking finance rather than production as the underlying organizational principle. This then gets coupled with an extreme confidence in the leadership – parallel to the near-awe everyone seems to have of the verdicts of 'the finance market' nowadays. (Jones 2013)

Corporate philanthropy and philanthro-business are therefore symptoms of what many perceive as a 'state crisis' with its suggested solutions being a symptom or expression of the general marketization that most non-profit enterprises and activities experience at present, where the devaluation of non-markets go hand in hand with a near-total confidence in the market, the innovative entrepreneur and the efficient leader as the new 'social fixer'. In a report by the famous entrepreneur Bill Drayton, *Everyone a Changemaker* (effectively mobilizing the neoliberal over-confidence in the individual, everyone is an individual changemaker, while obscuring the structural limitations differentiating the possibilities of 'everyone') it states that some good work was performed prior to the present age but all systems were change averse, "hence the squalor of the social sector. Relative performance declining at an accelerating change." Luckily that all changed: "It was only around 1980 that the ice began to crack and the social arena as a whole made the structural leap to this new entrepreneurial competitive architecture." (Drayton 2006, 5).

It is hardly surprising that the very precisely dated shift coincides with the neoliberal turn and the massive onslaught on the public sector.

The fetishism of numbers, indicators, and measurements is not innocent. It is performative in the sense that it creates the world it purports to describe. While problematic in the business world, it is damaging in the non-profit world where many of the goals are intangible and hard to measure. At present, the trend is to substitute civil society's intangible values with market or numerical values. However, non-profit organizations should be "mindful of the fact that not all desirable social outcomes can be easily or accurately measured. Instead, the goals of philanthropic work reach beyond concrete, instrumental targets set by a stern manager, and extend to such intangible ideals as community, empowerment, justice, creativity, compassion, expression, preservation of legacies, or the like." (Jenkins 2011, 36)

Even more damaging in the marketization of philanthropy is the narrative of organizational failure due to non-market principles. The less anything resembles a market or a market actor the more deficient it is. Philanthropic organizations have been caught up in this market narrative and have failed to defend their history and values, both of which come out in no small measure from a distance to the market, from a no to the profit principle or the quick fix. It is because they didn't see themselves as a business, their volunteers as employees and the people they struggled for as customers, that they stayed 'in business' and did the work. I often come to the conclusion that Michael Edwards has formulated this in better words than I can myself, and so I give the word to him once again:

This is a very odd way to talk about groups that have cared for the casualties of every crisis and recession for a hundred years or more, kept communities together in good times and the bad, brought democracy alive in places very large and very small, protected the environment from continuous corporate degradation, pushed successfully for the advancement of civil and women's rights, and underpinned every successful social reform since slavery was abolished. As far as I can tell, the people who make such statements [that the 'old' philanthropic organizations are inefficient and useless] have never worked in groups like these, nor have they studied the achievements and history of civil society organizations, nor have they experienced the difficulties of tackling power and inequality on a shoestring and in the face of constant opposition. (Edwards 2010, 4)

Maybe the philanthropic organizations should rediscover their non-market roots. It doesn't even have to be anti-market, just a reflection on their grounding in civil society and the values, histories and struggles that arise from that, as opposed to from the market, evaluations, spreadsheets and related funding. From the market and the profit principle one should expect consumer products at affordable prices, but it would be a folly to also expect societal cohesion, justice, equality, or even love.

7

The not so Secret Millionaire: Plutocharity

One of the most high-profile and mediatized expressions of philanthropic capitalism is billionaire philanthropy where extremely wealthy individuals donate extravagant sums of money to charity. The best known are Bill Gates, Warren Buffet, and George Soros. The wealthy seem to have always given to some form of charity, often as an as integrated part of being rich, such as throwing grand dinners and stock-piling mansions with art (Jackson 2008). However, something qualitatively new seems to have occurred in the world of plutocharity (Lloyd 1993; Shershow 2005, 133-5; Handy 2007) that can be illustrated by the TV-series *The secret millionaire* where a rich person goes undercover as an average Joe to meet some of society's poor and ends up giving a large sum of money to people he has met. In a Danish episode of the series, the trailer reads:

> *In 'The secret millionaire' Carsten Mikkelsen says goodbye to the jet-set life style in Ibiza to go undercover for ten days in one of Denmark's most crime ridden cities – Hoeje Kolstrup in the municipality of Aabenraa. He has to live as an unemployed newcomer in a concrete ghetto, but is really on the search for projects to give money to. It becomes a journey where Carsten gets closer to reality's problems of poverty and violence. But it also becomes a meeting between people struggling to make a difference for others. A meeting which creates the foundation for new friendships and which Carsten in the end rewards with money from his own pocket.*
> *(http:/omtv2.tv2.dk, August 31, 2008)*

In manifestations of philanthropic capitalism like *The Secret*

Millionaire a distinction is enacted between the worthy poor and the entitled and caring rich and a claim is illustrated, namely that charity is about the rich transforming individual lives. Social conditions are turned on their head, the rich person is shown to be the one earning his or her riches through hard work and dedication and the problems of the poor can be alleviated through a cheque (Nunn & Biressi 2014). This series exposes nicely a significant problem in all charity: the difference between the giver and the receiver, not only during the charitable act – which gives us the ethical dilemmas of charity – but also before and after – giving us its structural issues. More importantly though, is the mention of the emotional affect which is a constant refrain in particularly billionaire and celebrity philanthropy. It is no longer enough to just give lavishly (often after one's death) and get something named after you, like in the good old days of classical billionaire charity. Now, you have to go out, feel a moral obligation and an emotional attachment to the ones receiving the charity. The dominant trend now is to get personally involved in the charitable acts, to use not only one's money but also one's time and competencies. One has to feel, engage, and participate. *The Secret Millionaire* shows millionaires as entitled to their wealth and are positioned as both exceptional (in business skill, spending and wealth) and as ordinary (in their ability to care).

This is also evident in the pledges listed on The Giving Pledge website where the personal motivation is at the center. The Giving Pledge started by Bill Gates and Warren Buffet "is an effort to invite the wealthiest individuals and families in America to commit to giving the majority of their wealth to philanthropy" (http://givingpledge.org).

There is, as Kavita Ramdas rightly notes, something unnerving in the fact "that the more unequal the world gets, the more the public is being invited to celebrate a cherished few who benefit from this condition of inequality." (Ramdas 2011, 394). Why celebrate that people give away what they can't possibly spend in a lifetime or two?

As seen in corporate philanthropy, a significant reason for getting into charity is the alleged inefficiency of the classical approaches to helping others. The discrepancy between one's moral and emotional engagement in other people's sufferings and the perception of the inabilities of classical approaches creates an obligation to invest one's time and money. Again, what triggers this expression of philanthropic capitalism is an anti-political conception of problem-solving. An employee at the Gates Foundation says: "We are sort of creating a post-UN world. People want to see quicker results" and he even mentions its democratic nature as one of the reasons for its incompetencies (quoted from Beckett 2010). This connects perfectly with the general devaluation of democratic procedures among the economic and political elites, appointing technocratic bankers to heads of states and looking envious to China as a place of genuine decision making power.

Plutocharity is the most extreme version of the present confidence in the 'super-competent individual', the leader, manager or celebrity, as opposed to the politician (Fridell & Konings 2013). This individual has proven his or her worth on the market – the measure of all things – and this market competence is now considered a universal competence applicable across the full spectrum of society, including philanthropy (Freeland 2012). Listen to Warren Buffett thinking out loud:

What if you had three percent or something like that of the corporate income tax totally devoted to a fund that would be administered by some representatives of corporate America to be used in intelligent ways for the long-term benefit of society? This group – who think they can run things better than government – could tackle education, health, et cetera, or other activities in which government has a large role [...] If there are things to be done in society that the market system doesn't naturally lead to, something like this would be a supplement to the invisible hand. It would be a second hand that would come down for society – administered in a businesslike manner – and it might be interesting to see what a system like that might produce. (in Gates & Buffett 2009, 23)

The plutocrat mimicking the over-competent individual the most is Richard Branson (wonderfully exposed as anything but competent in Bower 2014). In his sort of philanthrocapitalist book, *Screw Business as Usual*, Branson carefully documents everyone who has ever said he was great, narrating himself the admiring gaze he clearly anticipates from everyone around him. Not to be outdone by anyone, while not really contributing anything, he flashes the concept of Capitalism 24902 as his version of philanthropic capitalism, and then says:

Describing my philanthropic methods somebody recently said: 'Oh Richard, well yes he does things differently.' I would like to think that they meant that I don't donate cash willy-nilly, without questioning who is getting their hands on it and what they're using it for. I run Virgin Unite [his charity enterprise] just as I would any other business, making sure that our investments have the best possible social and environmental return. (Branson 2011, 9)

Going on about how people love him and how he changes lives, he dreams of ways to "turn typical corporate philanthropy upside down, moving away from solely the 'golden cheque' philosophy to becoming a true partner for front-line organiza-tions and leveraging absolutely everything we possess[ed] in order to drive change." (Ibid., 31) What is this new, innovative approach? It is "to do what Virgin does best and go out and find the gaps, issues that no one else would touch, so that we could work with partners to come up with entrepreneurial solutions." (Ibid., 32) Disregarding the self-serving hyperbole, the innovative approach is basically just business as usual, evidenced on the next page, "you should run charity like a business." (Ibid., 33)

Branson is clearly trapped in his own self-image of a daring adventurer charging at the old, industrial fortresses, unable to see that he is just another businessman. Plutocharity becomes one more way to image himself something else, and something braver, and to project the image, so often documented in this book, of 'going native' with ordinary people, of being just one of us going up against the powers that be, while in that move demarcating his tremendous distance from the rest of us. Coming down to us is all about the movement, demonstrating the mobility reserved for the rich and powerful who are able to choose where to locate themselves (documented in the book and books like this in the ever-changing geographical places they are, the access they have to everyone and everything, and in the constant listing of ordinary and extraordinary people who they meet).

Charity has become a distinction marker of the super-rich. Lists of donations are printed in newspapers and blogs, charity events are power-meetings, knowing who to support is now as equal a super-rich competence as knowledge of fine wine or whatever. It is one more thing marking them out from everyone else. Consumer society has softened the consumption divide between the super-rich and the rest but the extravagant donation, catching that headline, popping up on the generosity charts, is for the few only. Giving much away is one way to demonstrate superiority: 'I can do without that which you can't even dream about. I can do this extravagant giving and still have everything I want.'

Plutocharity has received a lot of media attention, not least because it is often flamboyant individuals giving huge amounts of money and promising grand and quick results. There is an almost potlatch dimension to this extravagant giving (Phillips 2008). It echoes ancient divinity, in this case self-divinity, counting on the awe of the spectator created by the excess.

However, plutocharity is not first and foremost an expression of extreme charity but of absurd inequality. Witness the subtitle of a recent boon on philanthropy *How the Wealthy Give, and What It Means for Our Economic Well-Being* (Acs 2013). The wealthy are cast as the potent makers of the well-being of the rest of us, commanding the economy and destiny of everyone else. This kind of argumentation is also dependent upon a notion of the wealthy as generous, whereas a lot of studies point to a significant correlation between wealth and egotism. Actually it's the least affluent parts of the population who give the most (3.2% of the income from the bottom twenty percent of Americans compared to 1.3% for the top twenty percent) and who give to charities serving people in real need rather than to already wealthy art galleries, museums, universities and other such things truly not meriting the charity label (Manne 2014). However, one looks in vain for a discussion and recognition of all these anonymous everyday people and their giving among the celebrations of philanthropic capitalism, possibly because they are all about that old-fashioned solidarity thing.

The significant fact to observe is the relation between new forms of charity and a massive and growing inequality. It may, on a personal level, be motivated by moral concerns but on a structural level a way to manage legitimacy and possibly also the social challenges of extreme inequality. It is not that one thinks one has not earned the money but what Thorstein Veblen a hundred years ago called 'conspicuous consumption' must now be supplemented by conspicuous non-consumption in the form of charity in order for the still extravagant consumption to be both legitimate and enjoyable.

There is no reason to be in awe of the mega-donations of the super-rich or to expect much from their super-human self-professed abilities. Rather than celebrate their generosity, one should question the worth of their actions. Are the means doled out to charity earned in an ethical way, or are we asked to be satisfied with the handouts from a system screwing up our societies and the planet? The super-rich have not become so through super-human effort but largely through permissive business and tax regimes and the only adequate response to the problems philanthropic capitalism professes to address is to reorder that regime, starting with finance speculation, a lot of which should simply be outlawed as dangerous and damaging. When people like Warren Buffett or George Soros ask to be taxed heavier we should of course oblige them, but we should also address the source of the funds taxed. "It is unrealistic in the extreme", says John Roemer, "to expect that wealthy capitalists will dispense as much wealth through corporate philanthropy as could be raised by a more redistributive system of taxation than we now have." (Roemer 2009, 156) However, it is also unrealistic in the extreme to expect that the social ills and injustices of this world can be solved through the heavy taxation of the ones profiting from an unjust system.

The World is Watching: Celebrity Philanthropy

The American actor George Clooney has sponsored with private funds a satellite to monitor troop movements in the south of Sudan to help avoid another genocide in the region. Everyone can watch the movements on the website www.satsentinel.org whose motto is "The world is watching because you are watching." This motto nicely summarizes the logic behind a fast growing trend of using celebrity status to generate attention on issues other than their marriage/divorce-cycles and to force action on pressing global issues. Clooney himself had been instrumental in securing the referendum that in January 2011 gave an overwhelming majority for secession of South-Sudan from the rest of the country (Avlon 2011) The world is watching because they are watching. And what the world is watching is not really poverty, disasters or disease but the celebrities watching whatever they are watching (Hollar 2007; Barker 2013)

Celebrity culture is big business. Celebrities in the entertainment business earn massively (and their sales, salaries and expenditures are often news stories in themselves); their celebrity status helps sell films, music, sport events; they have huge sponsorships and promote an endless variety of consumer goods; they sell news through the public nature of their lives; and they are themselves often flamboyant spenders. Everything connected with celebrities speaks money, massive amounts of money. They are, as Leo Lowenthal said already in 1944, "idols of consumption" rather than the industrial and political "idols of production" (Lowenthal 1961). Celebrities are fully integrated into the capitalist system and their celebrity status and function reflect not only our seemingly inexhaustible demand for someone to admire from afar but also the present configurations of the economy. I want to suggest that celebrities are a most visual *embodiment of capital* as it exists and flows today.

A strong connection exists between the new immaterial capitalism and its valuation of brands, reputation, story-telling in the so-called 'experience economy' (Pine & Gilmore 1999; Kapoor 2013 19-20) and the contemporary celebrity-culture. In both it seems the performative outweighs the qualitative, attention value versus use value. Where the economy was earlier connected to material production of ever more and ever cheaper, and where the valuation of a commodity was somehow attached to its primary or immediate utility, now it seems both economy and valuation are defined by immaterial processes of attention. Celebrities not only embody capital, they are also *brands personified*. Partially liberated from the old 'studio system' or 'star system' where business executives and studio heads dictated their every move, the celebrities are now like Nike, a name, a brand, an image with no production system behind it, which it is the business of the celebrity to maintain, defend and expand. Their name, personal life, and not least their body are the investment. The countless mentions of box office figures, places on the chart list and winnings in tournaments are nothing but the celebrity equivalent of the stock market news update on television. What is important are not really the amounts, just as the closing numbers on the stock market are not the real issue. What is at stake is the endless positioning of ups and downs. Is he moving up or down? Is she earning more or less than the co-actor? Celebrity-culture is symptomatic of a shift from criteria of qualification to ones of attention in and of itself as the gateway to celebrity (as evident in the reality-TV food chain of creating and forgetting 'celebrities'). It is increasingly celebrity status itself which generates celebrity status, rather than any admirable or praiseworthy acts. They perform for the adoring viewing public a hyper-individualism giving rise to the celebrity hero, the celebrity philanthropists talking truth to power or 'just doing it'. Celebrities act out a neoliberal subjectivity by the very way the celebrity system operates, celebrating the performer, the self-entrepreneur, the one making his or her life a business enterprise. Celebrity culture is one of the new life-forms in the immaterial economy, being played out on the red carpet and in reality TV-shows. What it does not offer is any justification of itself. It is there because we look, but it cannot answer why we should look and why they deserve our attention? Celebrity cannot answer why they should enjoy so extravagantly and why the rest of us should have a part in that luxury only as spectators. Again, we find philanthropy offering itself as one way to deal with the problem of legitimate inequality.

Philanthropy and celebrity were decisively united in the LiveAid-concert of 1985 where musician Bob Geldof brought together a string of artists for the biggest TV-event of its time. Charity was thereafter an ever more integrated part of what is expected of a celebrity (Poniwozik 2005). It often takes on a slightly comic or embarrassing form when celebrities wander about in places and problems they do not understand (but, honestly, do we know more? And does it not equally condemn us for watching not the catastrophe but the celebrity watching the catastrophe?). Or it can take on a more ominous form, as when the pop star Madonna brought home a child after a trip to Malawi in 2006 (Finlay 2011). This is not the place to discuss or criticize the celebrity contribution to alleviating the world's problems but what is of interest here is to look at celebrity philanthropy as yet another symptom of how the global attention-economy also needs an explicated moral dimension to be legitimate. It is becoming increasingly difficult to be just a celebrity enjoying the spotlight. The attention has to be redirected to something beyond oneself.

The Irish rock star Bono is probably the most famous of the celebrity philanthropists. He has cleverly used his rock star status to gain access to the halls of power from presidents to the Pope and he is a living advertisement of the initiative *Product Red* whose slogan is: "Buying (Red) Saves Lives" (www.joinred.com/red). The Red brand is added to already existing products (showing in perfect form the immaterial economy) and that part of the profits from buying Red products goes to a global fund combating HIV, AIDS, malaria, and other diseases. This expression of consumer philanthropy is sustained by the coolness factor of a rock star like Bono. A spiral of attention is created where celebrity status is exchanged for 'philanthropic attention' which is then fed back into greater celebrity status.

In a recent book on celebrity activism it is described as "the latest manifestation of the revised relationship between fame and achievement, whereby celebrities need to perform achievements (through activism and charity) in order to retain fame." (Tsaliki, Frangonikolopoulos & Huilaras 2011, 10). Celebrities are now free-floating self-entrepreneurs in an attention market. The fierce global competition among consumer brands and stocks are mirrored by the highly competitive fight for celebrity attention. "In today's rapidly changing world, celebrities feel pressure to keep their names in the news because it is a long time between movies or concert tours." Like the endless quarter reports of firms, promoting "a charitable or political cause allows celebrities to remain in the public eye and garner appearances on talk and entertainment shows." (West 2008, 78) Just like branching out into product endorsements, perfumes, clothing lines etc., celebrities need to get a foothold in the charity market in order to keep their name brand afloat. This is not to say that the charity work is pure self-promotion, far from it, but the connection between fame, attention, and charity is one no celebrity can afford to ignore.

The present mediatized celebrity system fits well with a certain heroic and compassionate charity narrative where the celebrity goes out into the world, preferably Africa, to meet the 'real people' of the world, to be moved by their stories, and decide to act. A strange gaze is created when celebrities look with pity at the poor and destitute. They look back in amazement and studied gratitude. And we look at them both. Who is really looking and who is looking at being looked at? There is even a website detailing celebrity giving called 'Look to the stars', again prompting the question: Who is doing all the looking that the celebrity system requires? Are these highly publicized celebrity charities telling us to give also, to get involved, or are they rather seducing us to outsource compassion and giving to the ones we have already outsourced the dream life to, the ones we have outsourced godlike agency to?

Celebrities perform a very important ideological function besides the more obvious one of legitimating consumer capitalism (Hayes & Seymour 2014), and that is to act as mediators between ordinary people and global capitalism. They are so far away from most people's everyday life, yet they seem so accessible. They are in the stratosphere yet all around us. "Celebrity", Philip Drake says, "...must at the same time seem obtainable (unlike, say, membership in the aristocracy) yet maintain a distance necessary to continue the aura of stardom." (Drake 2008, 440). Celebrities can mediate the distance between a global elite and a global capitalism on the one hand personified in group photos of heads of state, Davos summits, the big banks like Goldman Sachs or just the ominous world of 'global capital'.. Moving seemingly effortlessly in that distant and decoupled relation are the celebrities. Not only do they constitute a sort of meritocratic aristocracy, unlike a blood aristocracy, they also operate both on the global scene and on our homely screens. They are our access points to a world otherwise inaccessible. In order to perform that ideological function they must be both very close to us – we must feel addressed, part of their life, invested in their doings and personal lives – and far away. Celebrity philanthropy performs both those tasks. They participate in charities, travel to poor parts of the world, meet with ordinary people, and express commitment to people's struggling everyday life, but at the same time they fly in private jets, meet the presidents of the poor countries, and host a grand party.

Celebrities first replaced royals and then politicians as the ones feeling the pain of others in public. Like the plutocrats, giving is not enough. You have to feel, and no one feels as intensely or as publicly as celebrities. Again, this is the function that their mediating role performs for us. The distance from which a celebrity looks at people in need only really allows for pity. The fortunate gaze upon the unfortunate. This is not to say that politics and justice may not be articulated. It surely often is. However, the way celebrity charity is most often acted out is through the language and imagery of pity, of a celebrity feeling and a populace suffering. No matter the posturing of the celebrity of being just a human among humans, the only reason he or she is there and feeling is because celebrity has separated them endlessly and permanently from others, only to occasionally and momentarily in the charity setting rejoin them to us for a brief moment (Littler 2008; Barron 2009). Despite protestations and genuine motives, the celebrity/media-phenomenon doesn't really allow for anything else. Pity is really the only possible emotion in that situation. The distance and difference is enormous and anything other than pity posturing obscures the basic fact of inequality. When celebrities raise awareness of urgent causes a systematic pressure coming from the celebrity logic sets in, "the story ends up being not about Africans, but mostly about her [Angelina Jolie] – *her* experiences travelling there, *her* guilt, *her* sympathy." (Kapoor 2013, 22; Yrjölä 2009). Many celebrities know and manipulate this for good causes, but none can escape it, and it will inevitably reproduce the inequality that made it possible in the first place. For all the efforts to confront powers, celebrities can never confront the unequal logic of which they themselves are part. They can never truly confront the distance between the few and the many without ceasing to be celebrities. Making ironic gestures about being really just a person, or making fun at their own wealth and prestige, is something only the non-ordinary and the wealthy can do, and – as ideology critique 101 will tell you – it only exacerbates the distance while easing the conscience of the mighty.

Another dimension to the mediation between an inaccessible elite and ordinary people is directly related to the post-political condition. Many people feel more represented by celebrities than by their elected politicians. Celebrities both enact and subvert popular dissatisfaction with political elites. Dissatisfaction in post-politics is expressed by people's preference for celebrities rather than politicians, a preference often mentioned or alluded to by celebrities themselves. However, they also subvert the dissatisfaction, firstly by offering even more inaccessible solutions to the world's problems (celebrities on poverty safaris) and, secondly, by lending discredited politicians their aura, thereby aligning themselves with the present post-politics. In his critical exposé on Bono, Harry Browne clearly states and documents that Bono and celebrities like him are a story "about how those powerful people and institutions [they meet and are photographed with] are genuinely committed to making the world a more just and equitable place." (Browne 2013, 2). Celebrity philanthropy is parasitic on ordinary politics both by expressing what seems as an alternative to post-politics and by performing post-politics themselves, both moves alienating ordinary people from political and philanthropic action.

Celebrity activism is not a solution to crises of democratic representation. It is a symptom and possibly a radicalizer of the crisis. In an interview with *Rolling Stones Magazine* from 2005, Bono explained his role as a celebrity activist: "I'm representing the poorest and most vulnerable people. On a spiritual level, I have that with me. I'm throwing a punch, and the fist belongs to people who can't be in the room, whose rage, whose anger, whose hurt I represent." (Wenner 2005). The people 'who can't be in the room' stuffed as it is with celebrities, are not asked if they authorize this representation. This 'representation' is post-politics, post-representative democracy, at its purest. Democratic representation "is supposed to involve some kind of deliberative process, whereby a group of people choose a representative as their surrogate, advocate, or intercessor." (Dienst 2011, 117). However, not only does Bono circumvent democratic representation at the representational level, his description of his 'mandate' is also post-political, because Bono "does not claim to represent their interests, their perspectives, or even their hopes, but rather their 'rage, anger, and hurt'." (Ibid.). He 'represents' emotions not policies, bodies not subjects. Rather than representing political subjects, celebrities are perfectly placed to articulate and mediate emotions.

George Monbiot, among others, has noted that celebrities not only mediate. They are not merely or only relay stations between the population and the political and economic elites. They are also actors themselves and "have assumed the role of arbiters; of determining on our behalf" (Monbiot 2005) Celebrities, no wonder given the attention and amazement that surrounds them, assume and perform power. They are basically unelected leaders mistaking acclaim for consent. Monbiot is right to call them "bards of the powerful." They may criticize unrepresentative power but are so themselves. They may criticize inequality but are dependent upon it themselves. They may ally themselves with the poor in campaigns but their lives are spent rubbing shoulders with the rich and mighty. Post-politics is also spectacle politics, both in the sense that it's all for show and in the sense that it is performed as a show, and as Ilan Kapoor rightly stresses:

When charity work turns principally on spectacle and show, the tendency is to valorize dramatic stories and moral arguments, sound-bites and photogenic images, and quick and short-term solutions, often at the expense of a broad, complex, and long-term politics. When celebrities unilaterally represent the Excluded (the Third World, orphans, disaster victims, subaltern women, people living with HIV/AIDS), when they speak and 'witness' for them, the result is the construction of voiceless and passive victims. (Kapoor 2013, 115)

And let's add voiceless and passive spectators. Just like with plutocharity, it is the massive inequality, this time of attention rather than money, the differential access to media and popular attention, which enables the charity. The celebrity of the celebrities not only marks their difference from the rest of us. It gets inverted as an opportunity – possibly an obligation – to do good. The charmed life of the celebrities and our watching them gets bestowed a moral dimension otherwise lacking from a mediatized existence. The inequality in media attention is what makes this charity possible, and charity is part of what makes celebrity legitimate.

Lenders All:
Microcredit and the Poor Entrepreneur

In 1990, the French philosopher Gilles Deleuze published a small text updating Michel Foucault's thesis of the disciplinary society. Foucault had suggested that from the eighteenth century up until the beginning of the twentieth a particular societal logic centered round discipline had emerged and institutionalized itself. Disciplinary society operates through separation, incarceration, enclosure, surveillance, governed and disseminated through 'total institutions' like prisons, barracks, factories, schools and family, institutions shaped and authorized to create disciplined subjects. However, Deleuze says, Foucault realized that this societal logic, having itself superseded societies of sovereignty, met the limit of its functional logic in the middle of the twentieth century. The crisis of institutions and discipline gave way to a new logic, the logic of control. Unlike the disciplinary society where the subject passed from institution to institution each entailing a particular role as student, soldier, worker etc., the control society is characterized by constant development. The stable and demarcated in the disciplinary society gives way to the fluid and transformative in the society of control. Subjectivation no longer takes place in prearranged setups with specified demands (think qualifications authorized through examinations) but in ever-changing connections and self-manip-ulations (think lifelong learning, competencies, entrepreneur of your own life, 'be the change').

"Man," Deleuze writes, "is no longer man enclosed, but man in debt." (Deleuze 1992, 6) Unlike the externally enforced disci-plining created through institutions and commandments that characterized the society of control, subjectivation through indebtedness is created through the daily labor of molding the subject, which has been transferred from the institutions to the self. Subjectivation becomes self-work. Originally written in 1990, Deleuze felt the need to qualify and geographically limit his analysis to apply it only to the privileged fourth of the world population: "It is true that capitalism has retained as a constant the extreme poverty of three quarters of humanity, too poor for debt and too numerous for confinement: control will not only have to deal with erosions of frontiers but with the explosions within shanty towns or ghettos." (Ibid., 6-7)

Just as Deleuze updated Foucault, we need to update Deleuze. While he at a very early stage clearly saw what Maurizio Lazzarato later termed the making of the indebted man (Lazzarato 2012), he didn't see the oncoming massive debt subjectivation of the world's poor. Revealing possibly a hidden parallel to the bankers keeping the poor unbanked in his description of them as 'too poor for debt' in their 'shanty towns and ghettos', the remarkable thing since his essay is the exact extension of debt programs to the shanty towns, ghettos and rural districts of the world. The poor are no longer unbanked but indebted. Inequality is still rampant. Capitalism is still keeping a vast amount of the world's population poor but something has happened to the control of poverty. The erosions and explosions mentioned by Deleuze are still being countered with repression and exclusion, but the logic of the society of control is now being extended into the shanty towns and ghettos.

In *Life as Politics*, Asef Bayat describes a succession of perspectives on the poor starting with the 'passive poor' locked in a culture of poverty characterized by fatalism, traditionalism, criminality, lack of ambition, hopelessness, and a very low productive agency. This perspective is followed by 'the surviving poor' who are actively ensuring their survival through the options available: theft, begging, prostitution, street selling, squatting etc. displaying some, but nonetheless parasitic and unproductive agency. The next perspective is 'the political poor' who, unlike the first two, is not marginal but marginalized: economically exploited, politically repressed, socially stigmatized and culturally excluded. The political poor have an active but repressed agency. The final perspective on the poor in Bayat's description is 'the resisting poor' who exercise low-level micropolitics, street-level resistance and who are thereby able to carve out, negotiate and defend an existence. The resisting poor have an active but unacknowledged agency (Bayat 2013, 36-45). Bayat's description of changes in perspectives on the poor is convincing and demonstrates how various notions of agency have been put forward, either as lacking, unproductive, repressed, or unacknowledged, and that through these successive waves of thinking about poverty an ever more agency-filled poor have emerged. What is missing from Bayat's description is 'the entrepreneurial poor' who exhibit an active but blocked agency, who fail to become productive due to external conditions.

In the last few decades, a number of descriptions and practices have emerged that start from an idea of the poor not as a deficit-being (a classical strategy in the disciplinary society and lurking in the Deleuze quote above) but as a resource- and project-being. That is a description of the poor as obstructed entrepreneurs; entrepreneurs because life as being poor requires creative and continuous effort to survive but is obstructed due to efforts that are not translatable to a legal or profitable result. The ordinary banking, property, and work system is closed to the poor, forcing them to channel their entrepreneurial energy into activities outside the official system. This view is summarized in a 2004 UN Report as *Unleashing Entrepreneurship. Making Business Work for the Poor* by making the poor into entrepreneurs (UN 2004) and in the process devaluing public or collective common efforts. Three prominent voices in the 'liberation' of the poor's entrepreneurial energy is the Bangladesh banker (and Nobel prize laureate) Muhammad Yunus, the Peruvian economist Hernando de Soto, and the Zambian economist Dambisa Moyo. All three of them draw in different ways on the neoliberal description of poverty, development, and aid. They are the subaltern versions of the Western model subscribing debt opportunities rather than redistribution, individual entrepreneurialism rather than collective state or union efforts, personal effort rather than structural change, integration into capitalism rather than the fight for decent work and pay conditions, acceleration and deepening of the capitalist system rather than its alternatives. Indebtedness becomes the gateway to progress.

Let's start by looking briefly at the most controversial and combative of the three, Dambisa Moyo, who in her book *Dead Aid* launches an all-out attack on aid programs. In the chapter on banking, where she explicitly draws upon de Soto and Yunus, there are some interesting shifts from the poor to the entrepreneur, evident for example when she writes that the 9.5 million of Zambia's 10 million inhabitants who have no formal employment "remained ignored by the banking sector. Enter micro-finance. The many thousands of would-be Zambian entrepreneurs finally had a way to secure capital to fund their businesses." Half a page later, this group of people – Moyo gives the example of a woman selling tomatoes by the road –, have become "the real entrepreneurs, the backbone of Zambia's economic future." The underlying rationality seems to be a parallel understanding of people and capital summarized in her concept of "unseen, dormant cash, which simply needs to be woken" (Moyo 2009, 128, 129, 137). The poor are slumbering entrepreneurs just waiting to be awaken by debt and turned into capital.

Hernando de Soto has argued for the need to convert the poor's illegal and precarious use of land into legal property rights in order to put that land up as collateral in a formal lending process. Again the language is one of liberating the potential within and turning dead matter into living capital, that is turning the efforts of the poor into marketable items and themselves into bank customers (1989, 162-81, 242-4; 2000, 4-6, 74). His ideas have been met with great enthusiasm, not least from neoliberal think tanks and politicians, for creating the conditions for rewarding personal effort and for creating the infrastructure of progress. However, the individualist focus and not least the blatant lack of results have also produced quite a severe critique (Mitchell 2005, 2007, 2009) which, however, does not seem to have harmed his reputation among neoliberals. His idea connects so perfectly with the truths of the day, with the prevalent entrepreneurial fetish, that it is immune from critique. It is considered as correct, no matter what the realities are.

Most important and hyped of the three is Muhammad Yunus and his Grameen bank. In the preface to the Danish version of *Creating a World Without Poverty* the then minister for development and member of a liberal party, Ulla Tørnæs, wrote that the book had a "liberalist message" because its answer to poverty "is to release and nurture the potential that the individual possesses." (Tørnæs 2008, 7) Never mind that that is not a message or value particular to the market friendlies. More important is the way in which she and Yunus concur in viewing human potential in market terms, making it a neoliberal message (Rankin 2001; Bateman 2010; Chang 2010, chap. 15; Mellor 2010, 75-8; Karim 2011; Roy 2012)

Embarking on the idea of microcredit is born out of the important observation that a large part of the world's population does not have access to basic financial services and that this non-access seriously hinders them in moving from a survival existence to a welfare level. Yunus quotes bankers whom he tried to interest in making loans to the poor of saying that "the poor were not creditworthy. They had no credit histories and no collateral to offer, and because they were illiterate they couldn't even fill out the necessary paperwork." (Yunus 2007, 46-7). He then sets up his own bank lending small amounts to villagers in Bangladesh. He several times mentions, as if to calm his well-banked readers, that indebtedness is an effective control mechanism. Contradicting the banking community's predictions, Yunus remarks that the "poor paid back their loans, on time, every time!" and they did this "through nothing but hard work, every day." (Ibid., 47, 48). Indebtedness is not about pleasure but work. It creates obedient workers rather than lazy hedonists. Yunus is discovering a lesson also learned when consumer credit was extended to ever new groups in the West from the late nineteenth century onwards, namely that "consumer and mortgage credit, far from accommodating idleness, locked working people into a schedule of repayments that served to intensify rather than loosen the disciplinary pressures on them." (Konings 2010, 11)

Yunus also looks at the poor as obstructed entrepreneurs and indebtedness as the means of converting their everyday activity into proper economic activity. Inventiveness, creativity, problem-solving, the entrepreneur is generalized as economic features of man when he writes that the "entrepreneurial ability is practi-cally universal. Almost everyone has the talent to recognize opportunities around them" and when they, through credit channels, "are given the tools to transform those opportunities", into capitalist recognized, marketable activity, "almost everyone is eager to do so." (Yunus 2007, 54). The linkage between devel-opment, debt and entrepreneurialism is remarkable: "The first and foremost task of development is to turn on the engine of creativity inside each person [...] Microcredit turns on the economic engines among the rejected population of society." (Ibid., 56). It is not proper jobs or land reform but a particular economization of individual initiative that 'turns on the engine' and releases the potential that turns out to be basically the aspiration of being a small shopkeeper.

While the inversion of the poor in terms of surplus rather than lack is a very positive development, it comes with the same problems (and purposes) as the shift in affluent countries from workforce to creative force, from co-worker to co-creator and the universalization of the entrepreneur. "Given the right circumstances", a report says, "the entrepreneurial spirit can be sparked within any society." (Brainard & LeFleur 2005, 4). What seems to unite the poor and rich country emphasis on the entrepreneur and the liberation of the creator within is less a matter of creativity however, but rather work. It is about turning the poor (through debt) and the worker (through debt and a 'personal development' ethos) into ever-more hardworking beings. It is, as Lendol Calder in his book on consumer credit quotes a bumper sticker: "I owe, I owe; it's off to work I go!" (Calder 1999, 303). Microcredit is a highly individualizing promise of prosperity through integration into the capitalist nexus of debt and work. Updating the old saying about teaching someone to fish and he or she will have enough to eat forever, it is now indebt someone and he or she will work forever. Microcredit is many things, some good some not so much, but it is always a way to ensure that the poor work. This used to be achieved through repression, paternal moralism, or hunger. Now, it is achieved through access to loans and the self-work of the indebted.

10

The Gospel of Inequality: Philantrocapitalism

In the third chapter of the *Communist Manifesto*, Marx and Engels write:

> *A part of the bourgeoisie is desirous of redressing social grievances in order to secure the continued existence of bourgeois society. To this section belong economists, philanthropists, humanitarians, improvers of the condition of the working class, organizers of charity, members of societies for the prevention of cruelty to animals, temperance fanatics, hole-and-corner reformers of every imaginable kind. This form of socialism has, moreover, been worked out into complete systems.*

Philanthrocapitalism, as the ideological explication of philanthropic capitalist practices, I would argue, is one of the most dynamic bourgeois answers to a situation perceived as problem – and crisis-ridden. Dynamic because it not only criticizes state efforts, bureaucratic administration, and ordinary politics – as a standard liberal-conservative position would – but also because it offers an apparently coercion-free, individual based engagement type solution. It claims to organize the solutions not merely on the market in terms of profit – which, again, would be a classical right-wing response – but rather locates its effort in the interstices between market logic and private morality. In that sense, it links up with the ongoing restructuring of the welfare state in their joint mobilization of 'civil society' individuals to solve community or global issues. Both developments are parasitic on a notion of politics as ineffective and promote a notion of the individual, albeit the professionalized individual (often through the market or profit logic) as the better and warmer approach to problem-solving.

Philanthrocapitalism is part of the present rediscovery of civil society, not as the place of public, yet non-state and non-market, interactions and deliberations but rather as the site of efficient problem-solving. Civil society is functionalized and in that process also de-democratized. It is, therefore, inherently anti-political because politics is identified as part of the problem and because solutions are deliberatively phrased in un- or anti-political terms. Even as billionaires like Warren Buffett lobby for higher taxes on the rich to fund state initiatives in education, health, and other public services, the philanthrocapitalist idea is basically a marketization-through-moralization and a de-politi-cization-through-counter-bureaucracy. Politics have failed, so it gets repeated endlessly. Markets and morality are all that's left. Luckily, they are basically just two versions of the same effort to do good to people.

This is most evidently the case in a so-called 'philanthrocapi-talist manifesto' written by the authors of the book *Philanthrocapitalism* with the subtitle *How the rich can save the world and why we should let them* (Bishop & Green 2008a, 2008b, 2010a; Bishop 2006, 2013). In the manifesto, the authors Matthew Bishop and Michael Green put forward a number of suggestions on how to integrate philanthropy with the workings of capitalism, but more importantly they identify the present as a "post-crisis fiscal wasteland" with a need for "radical surgery on our public services. The last decade has been a gilded era for the government, as a raft of public spending commitments from health and education to international development have been hailed as the solution to social problems. But those times are over." The framing of the problem betrays its purpose. Why is the fiscal problem the overwhelming demand and not the missing funds, or to quote Armin Schäfer and Wolfgang Streeck criticizing the austerity program that philanthropic capitalism has become part of:

Everywhere the diagnosis is not that public revenue is too low relative to the functional needs of an advanced modern society, but that spending is too high on account of irrational collective or opportunistic individual behavior. The cure, therefore, is more discipline in spending rather than paying taxes – except perhaps for the taxes paid by ordinary people, such as social security or consumption taxes. Consolidation is identified almost entirely with budget cuts. (Schäfer & Streeck 2013, 10; also Streeck 2014).

The state, Bishop and Green allege, cannot be trusted to "tackle the social challenges of the 21st century" and neither can "the charity sector" or "populist bashing of the rich." Instead, we need to "rewrite the social contract between the rich and the rest". They have "a responsibility to the rest of society" that goes beyond paying taxes, namely to "give back with their money and their skills". With that they can be "a dynamic, entrepreneurial source of innovation" – notice the ever-great hope in the entrepreneurial and the definition of development as innovation – and help to "build a more sustainable environment for wealth creation." (Bishop & Green 2010a). One can hardly overestimate the significance in their final description of what a healthy society would look like, a 'sustainable environment for wealth creation'. This is using the market model as societal description and it is basically a message to the rich that they can only stay rich – and richer than 'the rest of us' – by giving time and money to charity.

Philanthrocapitalism as the ideological explication of the activity of philanthropic capitalism, is not, they write, "a party-political issue. It is an opportunity to create a new partnership of philanthropists, businesses and social entrepreneurs with government." (Ibid.). Never mind the ideological claim of being a non-party issue. They are right in the sense that this hope in philanthrocapitalism is widely shared across the political spectrum (Bill Clinton has been touring with Matthew Bishop on precisely this issue). More interesting are the legitimating resources found in this claim of capitalism's profits and approaches as to the way to address global and local issues. In their 2008-book, there is a final chapter called 'The Gospel of Wealth 2.0'. In it they quote the Indian software giant Nandan Nilekani saying:

> *In a country with as much stark poverty and income disparity as India and which has just tentatively embraced free market ideology, it becomes all the more critical that the rich embrace philanthropy. It is not only the moral and ethical thing to do. It is also vital to making entrepreneurial capitalism acceptable to the people as the best form for the economy. The rapid rise of philanthropy amongst India's business leaders is the fork in the road between India becoming a modern equitable free market democracy or going back to a stultifying socialistic state.* (quoted in Bishop & Green 2008a, 257)

This linkage between inequality and entrepreneurial capitalism as well as the opposition between politics, on the one hand, and philanthropy and free market ideology on the other hand, is exactly at the core of my argument above and is the dominant idea behind philanthrocapitalism, both as to why it is supposedly badly needed at present and how it will answer that need. The morally just and the capitalist beneficial seem to converge in the call for more philanthropy.

In *Philanthrocapitalism*, "learned cynicism about wealth" and the imperative to tax is time and again repudiated in favor of a description of the super-rich as the ones with "the potential to solve many of the biggest problems facing humanity today". The new philanthropists "are trying to apply the secrets behind [their] money-making success to their giving" and they – as well as Bishop and Green "see a world full of big problems that they, and perhaps only they, can and must put right." They are "hyper-agents who have the capacity to do some essential things far better than anyone else." The solution "is in their hands." (Bishop & Green 2008a, xi, 2, 12, 13). Perhaps that is why almost all critique of the rich are dismissed, ridiculed, or just mentioned without any attempt to discuss their validity (e.g. ibid., 66-67). And perhaps that is also why we hear in incredible detail how, and not least how much, they give, but very little about what impact their giving actually has. It is all about the rich and their fabulousness.

One is struck by their confidence in business and business leaders (witness the whitewashing of Shell, Walt-Mart and Goldman Sachs, ibid., 180-185, 220-221). Publishing their book literally in the midst of the financial crisis, they write: "Yet in the past few decades, there has been a revolution in finance", true so far, "that has allowed a much deeper understanding of risk and generated more efficient ways of managing it." Really? "This has resulted overall, in a massive increase in the productivity of capital, the lifeblood of capitalism, and has benefited most of us, by driving faster economic growth, as well as handsomely rewarding its most capable practitioners." (Ibid., 76). Well, at least they got the last part right.

In a follow-up to *Philanthrocapitalism*, Bishop and Green published in 2010 *The Road from Ruin. How to Revive Capitalism and Put America Back on Top*. The book starts with a move known from many post-crisis books, "Capitalism as we knew it ended on September 15, 2008." (Bishop & Green 2010b, 1). What follows is then a critique of capitalist excess and a largely voluntary reigning in of irrational business exuberance. For all intent and purposes, capitalism as we know it. The finance crisis turns out to be not the start of something new but the return to something old, namely the civilized capitalism before the crazy years. The authors don't really fear capitalism. It will learn its lesson and go back to being nice. What they fear is government regulation: "Populist regulation of the banks, particularly of bankers' salaries, risks hobbling our economies with unnecessary bureau-cracy." (Ibid., 23).

Philanthrocapitalism turns out to be a preemptive strike against government intervention, "against ill-considered government plans to impose social responsibilities on businesses (a renewed danger in these times of rapidly expanding government)." (Ibid., 273; see Wilson 2014b). Capitalism works, they say, "because it taps into the widespread desire to become wealthier." So we can either reward those who become one with that desire or we can regulate and risk ruin and circumvention of the rules: "However, popular politically, restricting the ability of people in business and finance to earn way above the average would be a huge mistake, discouraging wealth creation and creating an incentive to waste resources in finding ways to get around the restrictions." (Ibid., 281). While they call our time the age of philanthrocapitalism, it turns out to be just another celebration of self-regulated free market capitalism with extreme wealth creation at the top and charity to the bottom.

Philanthrocapitalism serves here as a way to legitimate and perpetuate inequality and to derail any alternatives to capitalism. Running throughout their argumentation is a celebration of capitalist actors and a devaluation of state and traditional charity. The foremost danger in their narrative is not rampant inequality or material injustice but the danger of a new redistributionist activism on the part of politicians and publics. Generosity is not motivated by solidarity but by fear.

One is reminded of one of several essays and interventions seemingly taking inequality seriously but really just fearing unrest. In 2014, the self-professed ultra-rich "proud and unapologetic capitalist" Nick Hanauer addressed his "fellow filthy rich Americans" with the prediction that "the pitchforks are coming." (Hanauer 2014). Inequality's real problem, according to Hanauer, is its propensity to start rebellions. The fight for justice and equality is constantly painted in the colors of destruction and riot. "In fact, there is no example in human history where wealth accumulated like this and the pitchforks didn't eventually come out."

11

Ungrateful and Disobedient

Every society has dealt with the question of the morality of inequality (Wisman & Smith, 2011). My argument has been that philanthropic capitalism is one of the most important ways it is being dealt with morally, politically, and organizationally in a specific historical constellation of growing material inequality and economic transformation.

Pro bono is Latin and means 'for the common good' and it usually refers to professionals, like lawyers, using their expertise for free to help others. In the title of this book, it refers to a small pun on the rock star singer Bono and the purpose is simply to raise the question of what philanthropic capitalism represents. If it is more than the desire to help others, then what is this 'more'? The purpose has not been to expose, ridicule, or criticize philanthropic capitalist actors, to devalue philanthropy as paternalistic or ineffective, or to discuss the moral philosophical implications in helping others, nor finally to evaluate the actual effects of this activity (others have done that, Reich 2006; Singer 2006; Ruiz 2006; and not least Edwards 2008, 2010). The purpose has been to explore what all this pro bono-activity signifies when viewed within a grander societal framework, where capitalism steps in as the active instrument of philanthropy, where the development in capitalism enables new practices, where inequalities are rampant and growing, and where new oppositions to the global system seems to be mounting.

The economy is becoming dependent upon external qualities of the self whilst threatening its capitalist form. This is what is sometimes referred to as "communism of capital" where "the capitalistic initiative orchestrates for its own benefit precisely those material and cultural conditions which would guarantee a calm version of realism for the potential communist" (Virno 2004, 6.11). I'm reluctant to place the analysis squarely within this 'communism of capital' approach, as I fear it obscures how capitalism not only appropriates but also changes the appropriated. I would rather speak in continuation of Adam Arvidsson who investigates how "the most important source of value becomes the ability to appropriate an externality" (Arvidsson 2006, 9), in this case the moral and relational resources inherent in individuals. Like Arvidsson's work on brands, I have looked at philanthropy "as a capitalist institution, and not just as a cultural phenomenon." (Ibid., 14). Capitalism is trying to restructure its operational and legitimating set-up to address this general tendency to appropriate externalities, and I have argued that philanthropic capitalism should be seen as such an attempt, trying to address the problem of inequality on the basis of a manageable but also expanding version of 'moral capitalism'.

The main conclusion is that the various philanthropic capitalist ideas investigated above are different expressions of the same adaption to the demands of a capitalism where emotional, relational, cognitive and imaginative resources are not only mobilized but also valorized as the main productive force of economic practice. This new constellation can be called "cognitive capitalism" (Boutang 2011) or "immaterial capitalism" (Gorz 2010), the main point being that "personality and subjectivity" (Lazzarato 1996, 133), qualities of the self, are not only being capitalized, it is not only, and possibly not primarily, a move from inside the companies out, but it is rather the companies having to go beyond the internal profit logic, that is to the realm of everybody's daily life. The personal has become not only the political, as the 1970s slogan said. The personal has become everything. The personal, the emotional, relational and creative qualities of the self have become the guiding principle of private and collective organization.

Emotional responses turn inequality into a personal issue,

both for the fortunate and the unfortunate whose relation is mediated by charity and gratitude. However, we should repeat Oscar Wilde's rejection of gratitude and say: "*the best amongst the poor are never grateful*. They are ungrateful, discontented, disobedient, and rebellious." And so should be the rest of us too.

Let's take a final lesson from a talk-show at the Canadian CBC News Channel in January 2014. The topic was a story from Oxfam that the world's richest 85 earn more than the bottom half of the global population. Debating the issue was the libertarian entrepreneur Kevin O'Leary and the centrist journalist Amanda Lang. The exchange between them is not about philanthropy but it is all about inequality and about a liberal suddenly having to say stop and realize the amoral stupidity of both our current system and its cheerleaders. When Lang has mentioned the numbers O'Leary says:

O'Leary: "It's fantastic and this is a great thing because it inspires everybody, gets them motivation to look up to the one percent and say, 'I want to become one of those people, I'm going to fight hard to get up to the top.' This is fantastic news and of course I applaud it. What can be wrong with this?
Lang: Really?
O'Leary: Yes. Really. I celebrate capitalism.
Lang: A person living on a dollar a day in Africa is getting up in the morning saying: 'I want to be Bill Gates.'
O'Leary: That's the motivation everybody needs. I'm not against charity.
Lang: 'The only thing between me and that guy is motivation. I just need to pull up my socks. Oh wait, I don't have socks'.
O'Leary: Don't tell me that you want to redistribute wealth again, that's never gonna happen.
Lang: Or you take a simple step like this which is neither good nor bad, it's just a fact …
O'Leary: It's a celebratory stat. I'm very excited about it. It's

wonderful to see it happen. I tell kids every day …

Lang: You know what. I'm just gonna …

O'Leary: What's wrong with this?

Lang: One possible response to it …

O'Leary: If you work hard, you might be stinking rich one day.

Lang: We're talking about people in extreme, abject poverty. That's how you get three and a half billion…

O'Leary: No, we're not. We're talking about very rich people.

Lang: No! … I will tell you later what to say about this.

Acknowledgements

Family, friends, and colleagues are the ones to whom we truly owe a debt. Our relations to them are a daily refutation of the neoclassical and neoliberal claim of self-interested human beings. Love, work, and community mark out spheres alien to theories of self-interest. They constitute a spontaneous communism of 'to each according to his and her needs, from each according to his or her abilities'. That is no theoretical thought but a daily practice. Those relations are structures – for good and bad – created through solidarity, not pity or charity. It is to them that we say 'thank you', even though we do not need to uphold civil niceties. Still, thanks are in order, if for nothing else then to remind us that what we do and are, we owe to them too.

This book started out as a chapter in a Danish volume on the many faces of capitalism from 2012. I want to thank my co-editing colleagues Morten Raffnsøe-Møller, Thomas Vinther Larsen, and Ejvind Hansen as well as Christian Olaf Christiansen with whom I wrote my first pieces of capitalism critique and who has always intelligently and patiently read and commented on my stuff even though I suspect that he thinks I'm too radical. Christian is part of my research project called the History of Economic Rationalities funded by the Velux Foundation, of which Jakob Bek-Thomsen and Stefan Gaarsmand Jacobsen are also members. I thank them too for an endless amount of helpful suggestions through the years. From a book chapter it went into a conference paper and from there to an article in the journal *Ephemera* in 2013. I thank the anonymous review and the editors, especially Anna-Maria Murtola, who deeply engaged in the arguments and pushed me in all the right directions. The jump from article to book came as a result of a research stay at Goldsmith's in London in 2014, kindly secured and hosted by Sanjay Seth and Francisco Carballo. And that brings me to the final thanks, to my friends and family who keep asking: 'what is it exactly that you do?' pushing me to leave the safe confines of theory and to make my work explainable and, hopefully, relevant to them too. It is a true privilege to have great colleagues, friends, and family to engage with in endless dialogue. I thank them all.

Bibliography

Acs, Zoltan J. (2013). *Why Philanthropy Matters. How the Wealthy Give, and What It Means for Our Economic Well-Being*, Princeton & Oxford: Princeton University Press.

Arendt, Hannah (1965). *On revolution*, London: Penguin.

Arviddson, Adam (2006). *Brands. Meaning and value in media culture*, London & New York: Routledge.

Avlon, John (2011). "George Clooney: a 21st Century Statesman", *Daily Beast*, 21 February.

Barker, Michael (2013). "Celebrity Philanthropy: In the Service of Corporate Propaganda", chap. 7 in Rebecca Fisher (ed.), *Managing Democracy, Managing Dissent. Capitalism, Democracy and the Organisation of Consent*, London: Corporate Watch & Freedom Press.

Barron, Lee (2009). "An actress compelled to act: Angelina Jolie's Notes from My Travels as celebrity activist/travel narrative", *Postcolonial Studies*, vol. 12, no. 2, pp. 211-228.

Bateman, Milford (2010). *Why Doesn't Microfinance Work? The Destructive Rise of Local Neoliberalism*, London & New York: Zed Books.

Bauman, Zygmunt (2005). *Work, Consumerism and the New Poor*, Cambridge: Polity.

Bayat, Asef (2013). *Life as Politics. How Ordinary People Change the Middle East*, 2. ed., Stanford: Stanford University Press.

Beckett, Andy (2010). "Inside the Bill and Melinda Gates Foundation", *The Guardian*, 12 July.

Bishop, Matthew (2006). "The Birth of Philanthrocapitalism", *The Economist*, 23 February.

Bishop, Matthew (2013). "Philanthrocapitalism: Solving Public Problems through Private Means", *Social Research*, vol. 80, no. 2, pp. 473-490.

Bishop, Matthew & Michael Green (2008a). *Philanthrocapitalism.*

How the rich can save the world and why we should let them, London: A & C Black.

Bishop, Matthew & Michael Green (2008b). "Can the rich save the world? Interview with Matthew Bishop and Michael Green", *Alliance Magazine*, October, www.alliancemagazine.org/node/1584.

Bishop, Matthew & Michael Green (2010a). "The Philanthro-capitalist Manifesto", www.philanthrocapitalism.net/2010/01/the-philanthrocapi-talist-manifesto/.

Bishop, Matthew & Michael Green (2010b). *The Road from Ruin. How to Revive Capitalism and Put America Back on Top*, New York: Crown Business.

Boltanski, Luc & Ève Chiapello (2005). *The New Spirit of Capitalism*, London & New York: Verso.

Boutang, Yann Moulier (2011). *Cognitive Capitalism*, Cambridge: Polity.

Bower, Tom (2014). *Branson. Behind the Mask*, London: Faber & Faber.

Brainard, Lael & Vinca LaFleur (2005). *Expanding Enterprise, Lifting the Poor. The Private Sector in the Fight against Global Poverty*, Washington, DC: Brookings.

Branson, Richard (2011). *Screw Business as Usual*, London: Random House.

Brei, Vinicius & Steffen Böhm (2011). "Corporate social responsi-bility as cultural meaning of management: a critique of the marketing of 'ethical' bottled water", *Business ethics: A European review*, vol. 20, no. 3, pp. 233-252.

Browne, Harry (2013). *The Frontman: Bono (In the Name of Power)*, London & New York: Verso.

Buffett, Peter (2013). "The Charitable-Industrial Complex", *New York Times*, 26 July.

Byrne, John A. (2002). "The New Face of Philanthropy", *Business Week*, 2 December.

Calder, Lendol (1999). *Financing the American Dream. A Cultural History of Consumer Credit*, Princeton & Oxford: Princeton University Press.

Carnegie, Andrew (2006). *'The Gospel of Wealth' Essays and Other Writings*, London: Penguin.

Cassidy, John (2010). "What Good is Wall Street? Much of What Investment Bankers Do is Socially Worthless", *The New Yorker*, 29 November.

Chang, Ha-Joon (2010). *23 Things They Don't Tell You about Capitalism*, London: Penguin.

Chiapello, Eve (2013). "Capitalism and Its Criticisms", chap. 3 in Paul du Gay & Glenn Morgan (eds.), *New Spirits of Capitalism? Crises, Justifications, and Dynamics*, Oxford: Oxford University Press.

Christie, Nils (1986) "The ideal victim", pp. 17-30 in Ezzat A. Fattah (ed.), *From crime policy to victim policy*, Basingstoke: Macmillan.

Clinton, Bill (2007). *Giving. How Each of Us Can Change the World*, New York: Alfred A. Knopf.

Crook, Clive (2009). "The Problem with Gates: Do As I Say, Not As I Did", pp. 110-114 in Michael Kinsley (ed.), *Creative Capitalism. A Conversation with Bill Gates, Warren Buffett and other Economic Leaders*, London: Simon & Schuster.

Crouch, Colin (2011). *The Strange Non-Death of Neoliberalism*, Cambridge: Polity Press.

Davies, William (2014). *The Limits of Neoliberalism. Authority, Sovereignty and the Logic of Competition*, Los Angeles: Sage.

de Soto, Hernando (1989). *The Other Path. The Invisible Revolution in the Third World*, London: I.B. Tauris.

de Soto, Hernando (2000). *The Mystery of Capital. Why Capitalism Triumphs in the West and Fails Everywhere Else*, London: Bantam Press.

Dienst, Richard (2011). *The Bonds of Debt*, London & New York: Verso.

Drake, Philip (2008). "From Hero to Celebrity: The Political Economy of Stardom", chapter 18 in Susan J. Drucker & Gary Gumpert (eds.), *Heroes in a Global World*, Cresskill: Hampton Press.

Drayton, Bill (2006). *Everyone a Changemaker. Social entrepreneurship's ultimate goal*, Ashoka Innovations & MIT Press.

du Gay, Paul (1994). "Making up managers: bureaucracy, enterprise and the liberal art of separation", *British Journal of Sociology*, vol. 45, no. 4, pp. 655-674.

du Gay, Paul (2000). *In Praise of Bureaucracy: Weber, Organization, Ethics*, London: Sage.

Deleuze, Gilles (1992). "Postscript on the Societies of Control", *October*, vol. 59, winter, pp. 3-7.

Deutsch, Claudia H. (2006). "Lessons in Management From the For-Profit World", *The New York Times*, 13 November.

Edwards, Michael (2008). *Just Another Emperor? The Myths and Realities of Philanthrocapitalism*, London: Demos.

Edwards, Michael (2010). *Small Change. Why Business won't Save the World*, San Francisco: Berrett-Koehler.

Eikenberry, Angela M. & Jodie Drapal Kluver (2004). "The Marketization of the Nonprofit Sector: Civil Society at Risk?", *Public Administration Review*, vol. 64, no. 2, 2004, pp. 132-140.

Farrell, Nathan (2012). "Celebrity Politics: Bono, Prudct (RED) and the Legitimising of Philanthrocapitalism", *British Journal of Politics and International Relations*, vol. 14, pp. 392-406.

Finlay, Graham (2011). "Madonna's Adoptions: Celebrity Activism, Justice and Civil Society in the Global South", in Liza Tsaliki, Christos Frangonikolopoulos & Asteris Huilaras (eds.), *Transnational Celebrity Activism in Global Politics. Changing the World?*, Bristol & Chicago: Intellect.

Fleming, Peter (2009). *Authenticity and the Cultural Politics of Work: New Forms of Informal Control*, Oxford: Oxford University Press.

Foster, Lauren (2007). "A Businesslike Approach to Charity",

Financial Times, 10 December.

Foucault, Michel (2008). *The Birth of Biopolitics*, Houndmills: Palgrave Macmillan.

Frank, Thomas (1997). *The Conquest of Cool. Business Culture, Counterculture, and the Rise of Hip Consumerism*, Chicago & London: University of Chicago Press.

Frank, Thomas (2000). *One Market Under God. Extreme Capitalism, Market Populism, and the End of Economic Democracy*, New York: Anchor.

Frank, Thomas (2012). *Pity the Billionaire. The Hard-Times Swindle and the Unlikely Comeback of the Right*, London: Harvill Secker.

Freeland, Chrystia (2012). *Plutocrats. The Rise of the New Global Super Rich and the Fall of Everyone Else*, London: Allen Lane.

Fridell, Gavin & Martijn Konings (2013). *Age of Icons. Exploring Philanthrocapitalism in the Contemporary World*, Toronto: University of Toronto Press.

Friedman, Milton (1951). "Neo-liberalism and its Prospects", 17 February, http://0055d26.netsolhost.com/friedman/pdfs/other_commentary/Farmand.02.17.1951.pdf.

Gates, Bill (2008). "Making Capitalism More Creative", *Time Magazine*, 31 July.

Gates, Bill & Warren Buffett (2009). "Bill Gates and Warren Buffett Discuss 'Creative Capitalism'", pp. 20-39 in Michael Kinsley (ed.), *Creative Capitalism. A conversation with Bill Gates, Warren Buffett and other economic leaders*, London: Simon & Schuster.

Giroux, Henry A. (1994). *Disturbing Pleasures. Learning Popular Culture*, London & New York: Routledge.

Gorz, André (2010). *The Immaterial. Knowledge, Value and Capital*, London: Seagull.

Graeber, David (2011). *Debt. The First 5.000 years*, New York: Melville House.

Hanauer, Nick (2014). "Ultra-Rich Man's Letter: To My Fellow

Filthy Rich Americans: The Pitchforks are Coming", http://topinfopost.com/2014/06/30/ultra-rich-mans-letter-to-my-fellow-filthy-rich-americans-the-pitchforks-are-coming.

Handy, Charles (2007). *The New Philanthropists*, London: William Heinemann.

Hanlon, Gerard (2008). "Rethinking Corporate Social Responsibility and the Role of the Firm – on the Denial of Politics", pp. 156-172 in Andrew Crane, Abagail MacWilliams, Dirk Matten, Jeremy Moon & Donald S. Siegel (eds.), *The Oxford Handbook of Corporate Social Responsibility*, Oxford: Oxford University Press.

Hanlon, Gerard & Peter Fleming (2009). "Updating the Critical Perspective on Corporate Social Responsibility", *Sociology Compass*, vol. 3, no. 6, pp. 937-948.

Harvey, David (2005). *A Brief History of Neoliberalism*, Oxford: Oxford University Press.

Harvey, David (2010) *The Enigma of Capital and the Crises of Capitalism*, London: Profile Books.

Hayes, Niamh & Richard Seymour (2014). "Philanthropic Poverty", *Jacobin Magazine*, www.jacobinmag.com/2014/11/philanthropic-poverty.

Heelas, Paul & Paul Morris, eds. (1992). *The Values of the Enterprise Culture. The Moral Debate*, London & New York: Routledge.

Hoffman, Kurt (2008). "Placing Enterprise and Business Thinking at the Heart of the War on Poverty", in William Easterly (ed.), *Reinventing foreign aid*, Cambridge: MIT Press.

Hollar, Julie (2007). "Bono, I Presume? Covering Africa Through Celebrities", *Extra!*, 1 May, http://fair.org/extra-online-articles/bono-i-presume/.

Hopgood, Stephen (2008). "Saying 'No' to Wall-Mart? Money and Morality in Professional Humanitarianism", chap. 4 in Michael Barnett & Thomas G. Weiss (eds.), *Humanitarianism in Question. Politics, Power, Ethics*, Itacha & London: Cornell University Press.

Hume, Neil (2011). "God bless income disparity", *Financial Times Alphaville*, 17 November, http://ftalphaville.ft.com//2011/11/17/751221/god-bless-income-disparity.

Jackson, William J., ed. (2008). *The Wisdom of Generosity*, Waco: Baylor University Press.

Jenkins, Garry W. (2011). "Who's Afraid of Philanthro-capitalism?", *Case Western Reserve Law Review*, vol. 61, no. 3, pp. 1-69.

Johansen, Lars J. (2010). "Velgørenhed goes to market", *Mandag Morgen*, 26 April.

Jones, Campbell (2010). "The Subject Supposed to Recycle", *Philosophy Today*, vol. 54, no. 1, pp. 30-39.

Jones, Campbell (2013). *Can the Market Speak?* Hants: Zero Books.

Kapoor, Ilan (2013). *Celebrity Humanitarianism. The Ideology of Global Charity*, London & New York: Routledge.

Karim, Lamia (2011). *Microfinance and its Discontents. Women in Debt in Bangladesh*, Minneapolis & London: University of Minnesota Press.

Katz, Stanley N. (2005). "What Does It Mean to Say that Philanthropy is 'Effective'? The Philanthropists' New Clothes", *Proceedings of the American Philosophical Society*, vol. 149, no. 2, pp. 123-131.

Keat, Russell & Nicholas Abercrombie, eds. (1991). *Enterprise Culture*, London & new York: Routledge.

Klein, Naomi (2007). *The Shock Doctrine. The Rise of Disaster Capitalism*, London: Penguin.

Klein, Naomi (2014). *This Changes Everything. Capitalism vs. the Climate*, London: Allen Lane.

Konings, Martijn (2010). "Rethinking Neoliberalism and the Crisis: Beyond the Re-regulation Agenda", chapter 1 in Konings (ed.), *The Great Credit Crash*, London & New York: Verso.

Lavrsen, Lars (2008). "Verden reddes ikke af ånd eller politik –

men af kapitalisme", *Information*, 8 February.

Lazzarato, Maurizio (1996). "Immaterial Labor", pp. 133-146 in Paolo Virno & Michael Hardt (eds.), *Political thought in Italy*, Minneapolis & London: University of Minnesota Press.

Lazzarato, Maurizio (2012). *The Making of the Indebted Man*, Los Angeles: Semiotext(e).

Lee, Jennifer (2006). "A Charity with an Unusual Interest in the Bottom Line", *The New York Times*, 13 November.

Littler, Jo (2008). "I feel your pain: cosmopolitan charity and the public fashioning of the celebrity soul", *Social Semiotics*, vol. 18, no. 2, pp. 237-251.

Lloyd, Tom (1993). *The Charity Business*, London: John Murray.

Lowenthal, Leo (1961 [1944]). "The Triumph of Mass Idols", in Lowenthal, *Literature, Popular Culture, and Society*, Englewood Cliffs: Prentice-Hall.

Manne, Anne (2014). "The Age of Entitlement: How Wealth Breeds Narcissism", *The Guardian*, 7 July.

Mellor, Mary (2010). *The Future of Money. From Financial Crisis to Public Resource*, New York: Pluto Press.

Miller, Peter & Niklas Rose (2008). *Governing the Present*, Cambridge: Polity.

Mitchells, Timothy (2005). "The work of economics: how a discipline makes its world", *European Journal of Sociology*, vol. 46, no. 2, pp. 297-320.

Mitchells, Timothy (2007). "The Properties of Markets", chapter 9 in Donald Mackenzie, Fabian Muniesa & Lucia Siu (eds.), *Do Economists Make Markets? On the Performativity of Economics*, Princeton & Oxford: Princeton University Press.

Mitchells, Timothy (2009). "How Neoliberalism Makes its World: The Urban Property Rights Project in Peru", chapter 11 in Philip Mirowski & Dieter Plehwe (eds.), *The Road from Mont Pèlerin. The Making of the Neoliberal Thought Collective*, Cambridge, Mass. & London: Harvard University Press.

Monbiot, George (2005). "Bards of the Powerful", *The Guardian*,

21 June.

Moyo, Dambisa (2009). *Dead Aid. Why Aid Is Not Working and How There Is A Better Way For Africa*, New York: Farrar, Straus & Giroux.

Munk, Nina (2013). *The Idealist. Jeffrey Sachs and the Quest to End Poverty*, New York: Doubleday.

Nielsen, Peter (2009). "Tid til velgørenhed", *Kritisk debat*, June, www.kritiskdebat.dk/articles.php?article_id=817.

Nunn, Heather & Anita Biressi (2014). "Walking in Another's Shoes. Sentimentality and Philanthropy on Reality Television", chapter 26 in Laurie Oullette (ed.), *A Companion to Reality Television*, Malden: Wiley Blackwell.

OECD (2011). *Divided We Stand. Why Inequality Keeps Rising*, www.oecd.org/document/51/0,3746,en_2649_33933_491478 27_1_1_1_1,00.html.

OECD (2014). *Policy Challenges for the Next 50 Years*, OECD Economic Policy Paper, no. 9, July, http://www.oecd-ilibrary.org/economics/policy-challenges-for-the-next-50-years_5jz18gs5fckf-en.

Olsen, Niklas (forthcoming). "Crisis and the Consumer: Reconstructions of Liberalism in Twentieth Century Political Thought". On file with author.

Osborne, David & Peter Plastrik (1992). *Banishing Bureaucracy. The Five Strategies for Reinventing Government*, Reading, Mass.: Addison-Wesley.

Payne, Christopher (2012). *The Consumer, Credit and Neoliberalism. Governing the Modern Economy*, New York & London: Routledge.

Peck, Jamie (2010). *Constructions of Neoliberal Reason*, Oxford: Oxford University Press.

Peck, Janice (2008). *The Age of Oprah. Cultural Icon for the Neoliberal Era*, Boulder & London: Paradigm.

Phillips, Mary (2008). "Tycoon Philanthropy: Prestige and the Annihilation of Excess", chapter 13 in David Crowther &

Nicholas Capaldi (eds.), *The Ashgate Research Companion to Corporate Social Responsibility*, Aldershot: Ashgate.

Pine, B. Joseph & James H. Gilmore (1999). *The Experience Economy. Work is Theatre and Every Business a Stage*, Boston: Harvard Business School Press.

Poniewozik, James (2005) "The Year of Charitainment", *Time Magazine*, 19 December.

Porter, Michael E. & Mark R. Kramer (2002). "The Competitive Advantage of Corporate Philanthropy", *Harvard Business Review*, December.

Prahalad, Coimbatore Krishnarao (2005). *The Fortune at the Bottom of the Pyramid: Eradicating Poverty through Profits*, Upper Saddle River: Wharton School.

Ramdas, Kavita (2011). "Philanthrocapitalism: Reflections on Politics and Policy Making", *Society*, vol. 48, no. 5, pp. 393-396.

Rankin, Katharine (2001). "Governing Development: Neoliberalism, Microcredit and Rational Economic Woman", *Economy & Society*, vol. 30, no. 1, pp. 18-37.

Reich, Robert B. (2006). "A Few Hundred Supernovas", *Prospect*, 2 October.

Richey, Lisa Ann & Stefano Ponte (2011). *Brand Aid. Shopping Well to Save the World*, Minneapolis & London: University of Minnesota Press.

Rimmer, Matthew (2010). "The Lazarus Effect: the (RED) Campaign and creative capitalism", chapter 12 in Thomas Pogge, Matthew Rimmer & Kim Rubenstein (eds.), *Incentives for Global Public Health*, Cambridge: Cambridge University Press.

Rodgers, Daniel T. (2011). *Age of Fracture*, Cambridge, Mass. & London: Harvard University Press.

Roemer, John (2009). "Just Tax the Rich", pp. 156-160 in Michael Kinsley (ed.), *Creative Capitalism. A conversation with Bill Gates, Warren Buffett and other economic leaders*, London: Simon & Schuster.

Roy, Ananya (2012). "Subjects of Risk: Technologies of Gender in the Making of Millennial Modernity", *Public Culture*, vol. 24, no. 1, pp. 131-155.

Ruiz, Nicholas (2006) "Gates, Buffet, or Fail-Safe Philanthropy", *Kritikos*, July, http://intertheory.org/gates-buffet.htm.

Sachs, Jeffrey (2007). "The Forbes One Billion", *Forbes*, September 21.

Schäfer, Armin & Wolfgang Streeck (2013). "Introduction: Politics in the Age of Austerity", in Schäfer & Streeck (eds.), *Politics in the Age of Austerity*, Cambridge: Polity.

Schwab, Klaus (2008). "Global Corporate Citizenship", *Foreign Affairs*, vol. 87, no. 1, pp. 107-118.

Shamir, Ronen (2004) "The De-Radicalization of Corporate Social Responsibility", *Critical Sociology*, vol. 30, no. 3, pp. 669-689.

Shershow, Scott Cutler (2005). *The Work and the Gift*, Chicago & London: University of Chicago Press.

Singer, Peter (2006). "What Should a Billionaire Give – and What Should You?", *New York Times*, 17 December.

Smith, Craig (1994). "The New Corporate Philanthropy", *Harvard Business Review*, May-June.

Smith, Greg (2012). "Why I Am Leaving Goldman Sachs", *The New York Times*, 14 March.

Streeck, Wolfgang (2014). *Buying Time. The Delayed Crisis of Democratic Capitalism*, London & New York: Verso.

Strom, Stephanie (2006). "What's Wrong with Profit?", *New York Times*, 13 November.

Strom, Stephanie & Miguel Helft (2011). "Google finds it hard to reinvent philanthropy", *New York Times*, January 29.

The Economist (2006) "The Business of Giving. Special Report: Wealth and Philanthropy", *The Economist*, 25 February, http://www.economist.com/node/5517605.

Tsaliki, Liza, Christos Frangonikolopoulos & Asteris Huliaras (2011). "Introduction: The Challenge of Transnational

Celebrity Activism: Background, Aim and Scope of the Book", in Tsaliki, Frangonikolopoulos & Huilaras (eds.), *Transnational Celebrity Activism in Global Politics. Changing the World?*, Bristol & Chicago: Intellect.

Tørnæs, Ulla (2007). "De fattiges forretning og forretningen i de fattige", preface in Muhammad Yunus, *En verden uden fattigdom*, Copenhagen: Information.

Virno, Paolo (2004). *A Grammar of the Multitude*, http://www.generation-online.org/c/fcmultitude3.htm.

UN (2004). *Unleashing Entrepreneurship. Making Business Work for the Poor*, New York: UN Commission on the Private Sector & Development.

UN Global Compact (2003). *The 21ˢᵗ Century NGO: In the Market for Change*, http://www.sustainability.com/library/the-21st-century-ngo#. VKPFOz90yP8.

Utting, Peter (2005). "Corporate Responsibility and the Movement of Business", *Development in Practice*, vol. 15, no. 3/4, pp. 375-388.

Yrjölä, Riina (2009). "The Invisible Violence of Celebrity Humanitarianism: Soft Images and Hard Words in the Making and Unmaking of Africa", *World Political Science Review*, vol. 5, no. 1, pp. 1-23.

Yunus, Muhammad (2007). *Creating a World Without Poverty*, New York: Public Affairs.

Waal, Alex de (2008). "The Humanitarian Carnival. A Celebrity Vogue", *World Affairs*, fall, pp. 43-55.

Weeden, Curt (2011). *Smart Giving is Good Business. How Corporate Philanthropy can Benefit Your Company and Society*, Hoboken: Jossey-Bass/Wiley.

Weisberg, Jacob (2006). "The Philanthropist's Handbook", *Slate*, 15 November.

Wenner, Jann (2005). "Bono: The Rolling Stones Interview", *Rolling Stones*, October 20.

West, Darrel M. (2008). "Angelina, Mia, and Bono: Celebrities and International Development", chapter 4 in Lael Brainard & Derek Chollet (eds.), *Global Development 2.0. Can Philanthropists, the Public, and the Poor Make Poverty History?*, Washington DC: Brookings Institution Press.

Wilde, Oscar (1904). *The Soul of Man under Socialism*, London: Private Print.

Wilkinson, Richard & Kate Pickett (2010). *The Spirit Level. Why Equality is Better for Everyone*, London: Penguin.

Wilson, Japhy (2014a). *Jeffrey Sachs. The Strange Case of Dr Shock and Mr Aid*, London & New York: Verso.

Wilson, Japhy (2014b). "The Jouissance of Philanthrocapitalism: Enjoyment as a Post-Political Factor", chap. 5 in Japhy Wilson & Erik Swyngedouw (eds.), *The Post-Political and its Discontents*, Edinburgh: Edinburgh University Press.

Wisman, Jon D. & James F. Smith (2011). "Legitimating Inequality: Fooling Most of the People All of the Time", *American Journal of Economics and Sociology*, vol. 70, no. 4, pp. 974-1013.

Žižek, Slavoj (2006). "The Liberal Communists of Porto Davos", *In These Times*, 11 April, www.inthesetimes.com/main/print/2574.

Žižek, Slavoj (2009). *First as tragedy, then as farce*, London & New York: Verso.

Žižek, Slavoj (2014). *Trouble in Paradise. From the End of History to the End of Capitalism*, London: Allen Lane.

zero
books

Contemporary culture has eliminated both the concept of the public and the figure of the intellectual. Former public spaces – both physical and cultural – are now either derelict or colonized by advertising. A cretinous anti-intellectualism presides, cheerled by expensively educated hacks in the pay of multinational corporations who reassure their bored readers that there is no need to rouse themselves from their interpassive stupor. The informal censorship internalized and propagated by the cultural workers of late capitalism generates a banal conformity that the propaganda chiefs of Stalinism could only ever have dreamt of imposing. Zer0 Books knows that another kind of discourse – intellectual without being academic, popular without being populist – is not only possible: it is already flourishing, in the regions beyond the striplit malls of so-called mass media and the neurotically bureaucratic halls of the academy. Zer0 is committed to the idea of publishing as a making public of the intellectual. It is convinced that in the unthinking, blandly consensual culture in which we live, critical and engaged theoretical reflection is more important than ever before.